Facing a Father's Feeling of Failure

Facing a Father's Feeling of Failure

By

Wayne N. Taylor

The Dark Arts of Business, LLC
Wayne N. Taylor: wayne@waynentaylor.com
www.waynentaylor.com

ISBN 978-1-105-86175-8
Published by: Lulu.com

Dedication

This book is dedicated primarily to my beloved daughter Ashley Marie Taylor February 27, 1998 - January 14, 1999, who taught me how to love, how to give back to others, and how to give a second chance. Additionally, this book is dedicated to every father who has lost a child and has been frustrated that no one seems to understand what you are feeling. Hopefully, this book will not only assist you but also assist those who are trying to understand what you are going through.

Forward

I was surprised when Wayne Taylor asked me to write the Forward to *Facing a Father's Feeling of Failure*. I could not understand what I had done to help Wayne navigate through Ashley's devastating accidental death and his courageous, emotional journey in search of understanding and healing.

I remember that we discussed Ashley's death and Wayne's reaction to her loss on several brief occasions in the three years we worked together. I also remember, Wayne and I were usually the first to arrive at work and would seek each other out, for what Wayne called his "Morning session with the Doc." It puzzled me why he described our morning talks like this. We usually discussed challenges we were having with students or professional staff, what we did on the weekend, or perhaps our dreams of what we would do when we retired from the Army. I never had any idea we might be in what psychologists call a "therapeutic relationship." For me, we were good friends who enjoyed each other's companionship and cared about each other, our students, and our families.

After reading Wayne's book, I now realize that something much more emotionally charged was occurring in him, and between us, than was apparent on the surface. Our relationship, and others like it that he describes in the book, was crucial in transforming Wayne's intense suffering into insight, forgiveness, acceptance and closure. The intellectual and emotional insights he gained in this process and describes in *Facing a Father's Feeling of Failure* can help all of us not only better understand the trauma associated with the loss of a child, but also our own personal traumatic experiences in general. *Facing a Father's Feeling of Failure* also offers us a way to help one another face feelings of failure and begin to heal.

I have never lost a child. However, after reading *Facing a Father's Feeling of Failure*, I have a much better understanding of what someone who lost a child might be experiencing as they journey through this loss. I really liked Wayne's circular diagram of his personal grief cycle and how he provided so many specific examples of his thoughts and feelings that brought this cycle to life. I also liked how he indicated that his cycle was specific for him, and while there are likely to be similarities in our experience of loss, each of us needs to find our own internal grief cycle that rings true for our experience. In addition, he indicated that his journey through grief was not sequential. He noted that he would take two steps forward and one step backward in coping with helplessness, anger, loneliness and questioning his actions. He also explained how he would be surprised by his reactions to events that reminded him of Ashley's death.

I believe we can all relate to much of what Wayne had to say when we reflect on our own traumatic experiences, including the death of a child. As I read through the chapters, I found myself going back to traumatic events I experienced in support of combat operations in Afghanistan and Iraq. I identified with Wayne's difficult journey through anger, betrayal, failure, guilt and loss. In that identification, I was able to gain more insight into my own struggles with war-related trauma. I also found that his ability to put his thoughts and feelings into a coherent and understandable framework helped me to make better sense my own apparently chaotic experience. What a relief! I also marvel at the courage Wayne had, to relentlessly pursue the truth of his experience. By doing so, he provided me with an example of courage and important emotional "sign-posts" to navigate along a frequently dark, frightening, and bleak road with renewed hope of seeing brighter light at the end of the journey.

In my personal and professional experience of encountering and helping others and myself through traumatic loss, I have found making the experience conscious and processing it in an active manner are essential to the promotion of healing. There are many ways to accomplish this process, one of the most common being dialogue with others. A friend and fellow professional colleague, Dr. Rich Tedeschi, has extensive experience helping others who have lost a child. He notes that helping grieving parents heal from the death of a child is like two fellow travelers who are walking on a mountain trail. They walk together; side by side as much as possible, so that one traveler does not get too far ahead or behind the other. Sometimes the trail is steep, while other times it is flat or downhill. Staying together, the travelers can provide each other with companionship and courage to make the journey successfully.

Like these mountain travelers, I have found that helping others through traumatic loss requires a good enough relationship so we can suspend preconceived ideas about how one should react to loss, by assuming that the other's experience of loss is unique and true for them. We do not want to get too far ahead of the grieving person by evaluating their experience, offering advice, or telling them how they should think or feel. We also do not want to lag too far behind them, as can happen when we fear becoming overwhelmed by their emotional pain and shut ourselves off from their emotional experience.

It can be hard to stay emotionally connected to our family members or friends during grief and the strong emotions that spring from traumatic loss. Instead of just being present with another, we have the tendency to want to *do* something to help the grieving person as our frustration mounts as efforts to help them do not come quickly. In fact, as *Facing a Father's Fear of Failure* points out, trying to do something for a grieving person can be counterproductive.

When Wayne and I had our "Morning therapy sessions with the Doc," I believe we were traveling together on this mountain road. Once more, I am reminded of the incredibly powerful emotional connections and subsequent transformation that can take place when unconditional acceptance, positive regard and integrity are present in a relationship. I did not do anything for Wayne. I was simple available and present for him in midst of our busy daily lives for an extended period of time.

Facing a Father's Feeling of Failure provides you with a real-life story of how one courageous individual decided to confront his recriminating beliefs, rage and despair, which were pulling him down in an accelerating destructive tailspin. Fortunately, he recognized that his life was out of control and, with the help of his family and friends, made a choice to pull out of his emotional tailspin and live life again. What Wayne, and many others in similar circumstances have done, is not easy, but it can be done. Wayne's example shows us that, even though we have lost a child, things can get better if we can muster the courage to consciously face the trauma. Wayne's example shows us that we can forgive others and ourselves for the precious life of our child that we can never get back. Wayne's example shows us that we can begin to come to terms with life. There is hope, and at a future point in time, we can be thankful we are alive and mark this occasion by celebrating our own birthday once again.

Brief Bio: Dr. Jeffrey Stolrow currently serves as a clinical psychologist supporting high-risk training for the Department of the Navy in San Diego, California. He is a retired Army Clinical Psychologist with over 20 years of Service, including four combat tours in Afghanistan and Iraq. Prior to joining the Army, he served for eleven years as a civilian mental health provider for Kaiser Permanente and other mental health agencies. Since 1979 he has worked with wide range of clients, many of whom were referred to him for varied types of trauma and loss. Dr. Stolrow is married and has two children and two grandchildren. He resides in Newport Beach, California.

Table of Contents

My daughter was 10 ½ months old, and above all she was the most precious person in my life. Unfortunately, it wasn't until her death that I began to realize and understand what love really was.

Introduction

Conversations about death are often one of the taboo subjects that most people choose not to discuss, because they are not sure how to respond or cope with the subject. The reasons for this vary from the subject becoming too real, to being too difficult for loved ones to discuss. Growing up, I heard religious individuals speak of death but more about the afterlife and what one may expect. In my home, my mother raised me with Christian beliefs, so the afterlife is what was discussed, but never death itself. From the time I was a child, I had attended wakes and funerals of friends and people in our church that passed away. At most of these events, I would hear people say that the individual who passed away was in a better place and that was to be some type of comfort for those who were stricken with grief and the grieving process.

When I left my home to join the military in 1992, I didn't really think of the emotional aspect of death or that death would be something I would see or deal with, unless the country engaged in war once again. My thoughts changed in 1993 when I was assigned as a member of the United States Army Third Infantry Regiment (The Old Guard) at Fort Myers, Virginia. As many are aware, The Old Guard are the soldiers who walk the Tomb of the Unknown Soldier in Arlington National Cemetery, and they are also the ones who conduct the majority of the burials in the National Cemetery. For three years, I had the opportunity to see families mourn as I participated in funeral and burial details. Yet again, I was not personally affected as the ceremonies were so regimented and those being buried had no personal meaning to me. Seven years later, when a traumatic incident in my personal life occurred, I was faced with more questions than I could answer or that others could answer for me.

In January of 1999, I was the proud father of Ashley Marie Taylor, my 10 1/2 month old baby girl. In December we celebrated her first Christmas. On New Years Eve, she stayed up to welcome in the New Year. With her first birthday approaching, the plans were being established to have a wonderful birthday party with friends and family coming down to celebrate. Without notice, a tragic accident occurred and my daughter passed away leaving me with feelings and questions that would go unanswered, that even my faith could not resolve. Attempting to cope with the death, my wife at the time sought out counseling and could not understand why I didn't wish to speak to a counselor. She had books on grief and dealing with death. As I perused my way through them, I became angry and could not find a book that was willing to discuss how I felt. However, seemed to tell me that I was supposed to feel. A book of that nature was not what I needed at the time. I became angry, took unnecessary risks, drank, contemplated suicide, and retreated inward bottling up my feelings away from everyone. As a method of coping, I began writing down how I felt, why I felt that way, and what it meant to me. For almost thirteen years I have sat down and attempted writing this book to no avail, until now. I now know I have to come to terms with my daughters death. I know that I have to stop being angry, and I know I have to stop being selfish.

This book is slightly different than those presented by psychologists, grief counselors, doctors, or others who have dealt with death and grief as part of their profession. This book is written from a personal perspective, part of this is my journey through the grieving process, and the journey that others like me have taken, whether successfully or not, when trying to come to terms and cope with the death of a child. Though the book discusses the different grief cycle I and others may have underwent when we lost a child, I believe this book may help others who have yet to find their way in dealing with a significant loss. The intent is not to tell you how to grieve, how you should feel, or what you should feel. Instead this book allows you to relate to others who have experienced similar feelings and may have found themselves in similar situations. The process itself is not easy, and many relationships don't survive, as mine did not. At the same time, I found a different perspective on life, reassessed my values, and used the lessons learned to strengthen a new marriage and family. Unfortunately, not everyone shares the same success, as every path is different.

Often people expect a time limit to exist for the process, and I will be the first to share that the time is solely up to you. People go through the grief process at different speeds, and learning to fully come to terms and cope with the loss can be extremely challenging. Though I may have come to some level of acceptance earlier in my life, there are still issues that I work through today. One that I currently face is that my daughter passed away the day before my 25th birthday. Twelve years later, I will now attempt to celebrate my birthday for the first time since her death. I could never allow myself to celebrate before, since I felt it was a betrayal to my daughter's memory. To me, it seemed like I was betraying Ashley and therefore part of my punishment and the punishment of those around me has always been to not acknowledge my birthday. Though my, now and forever, wife Christy and our children were patient over the years, they would occasionally bring up the idea of having a small celebration or acknowledgement of my birthday, to which I would dismiss immediately and retreat into my memory and relive that day repeatedly. Even as I press on to continue writing, I find myself drifting back to the small amount of time I had with her.

Initially, memories seem to be a curse. Having the ability to relive an event repeatedly can truly be both a blessing and a curse. Each time I think of a memory of her playing with a toy, going to her first concert, or sitting and having dinner at the table in her highchair, my mind immediately transitions back to her in her hospital bed. I remember seeing the doctor walk down the hall to tell me that there is nothing else that could be done to bring Ashley back to us. The playback reel in our mind becomes directly connected to our emotions, always presenting a challenge for one to overcome when they think of their loved one. The old adage, "time heals all wounds" is not necessarily true. We fight to cope and work our way through the memories, or we become numb from any feelings creating a callous for our emotions, or we eventually forget the details that are so vivid and emotional and then feel guilty for not feeling the same way years later. Whatever the case may be, time does not heal the fact that you lost a child and that a portion of you no longer exists. What does heal is knowing that the pain eventually lessens, life continues to move forward, and when you are ready to, you can commit to the grieving process in your own personal way. One thing to remember is that no person grieves the same, as each of us come from different backgrounds and experiences.

When does one find closure and how does one find closure? How long does the grief process continue and how do you cope with it? What is acceptable and what is not? How do you move forward and try not to let the past interfere or challenge you? As significant changes occur, does coping become any easier? What is there to expect? Why doesn't everyone else see things from my point of view or understand where I am coming from? Some of these questions, if not more, will go through your mind or the mind of your loved ones after the death of a child. I won't say I have all the answers, but I will tell you that I am going to share with you my experiences as I ventured down my own personal grieving process. The answers may not fit you, or they may have some commonalities. What I ask is that if this book even touches on one aspect of your grieving process, hand it (or even throw it) at those who want to know if your handling grief and tell them to read it. Maybe, just maybe they will understand that you have your own way of dealing with grief and will let you work through it, as you feel fit.

Chapter One
My Story

My life was far from perfect growing up. I was raised in what is now considered a typical American home- a divorced home. From the ages two to eighteen, I had the adventure of living and experiencing life with my mother, which is a book within itself. At the age of eighteen and a recent high school graduate, I decided to be all that I could be and joined the U.S. Army. Like many foolish young soldiers I went from dating numerous women to marrying one of them. The woman I married was also in the military, and to make things a bit more challenging she was active duty in the U.S. Navy. (For those unaware, marrying outside of another military service can be extremely challenging when attempting to be stationed together or in close proximity.) Being young, naïve, and not marrying for the right reasons began to put a strain on our marriage. After approximately two years of strain, we made the mistake of trying to have a child in order to grow closer. A little over nine months later, our daughter Ashley Marie Taylor was born. At that time I was both excited and hesitant as I wasn't quite sure if I was ready for a child. I'm the type of person who always has a need to be on the go (further strain on a marriage), and constantly looking for opportunities to challenge myself either physically or mentally. So, with a child on the way, I decided this was something I would learn to endure.

Like most new parents who did not have younger siblings to care for, we were nervous and cautious about just about everything. Luckily for us, Ashley was a great baby girl. Ashley only cried when she was hungry or needed her diaper changed, or so we thought. We weren't ready for the unexpected crying when she turned the bottle away and didn't need to be changed, frantically we tried to find out what was wrong, and then we realized she had begun teething. We acknowledged Ashley was a good baby. I ended up taking her for granted since she was only a baby and couldn't interact with me, so I chose to dive headstrong into my work. I began spending an average of twelve to sixteen hours a day at work, and since it was the military I was able to keep myself occupied seven days a week. (Again, not something that was helping the marriage.) In the morning I would walk by her room while she was sound asleep, and in the evening I may have made it home right when she was getting ready for bed, or after she had already gone to sleep. Occasionally, I would pick Ashley up from the babysitter, whose family were our friends for about 2 ½ years, and bring her home just in time hand Ashley off to her mother, who had just arrived home form work. Because she couldn't interact, I didn't find her that interesting, and as such I didn't spend much time with her at all. I kept telling myself, when she starts getting older, she will be fun and I can do more with her.

In January of 1999, when Ashley was only 10 ½ months old, I came home early on a Sunday evening and spent about a 2 hours playing with Ashley before she went into her nighttime routine. For the next two days I worked late, not because I had to, but because I chose to. The next morning (January 12th), I left for work at the usual 4:30 AM, off to tackle the world and confront the new challenges that the day would bring. I conducted my daily routine as usual, but forgot to turn my cell phone on. At 8:35 AM, I received a call in my office from my wife saying, "Ashley, something wrong, ambulance taking her to (and the name of the hospital)". I told her I was on my way, told my colleague that I had to leave, and sped off to the hospital. Dressed in my military uniform, I was only halfway on the highway between Fort Bragg and the hospital when I was overcome with a sudden sinking feeling. With that feeling came the instant realization that my daughter had died.

Arriving at the hospital, a member of the hospital staff escorted me to a private room. I knew the purpose of these private waiting rooms. Prior to enlisting in the military, I had the opportunity to attend the Emergency Medical Technician course, where I had seen similar rooms used when families were to be notified of unfortunate information. I knew that being escorted to that private room confirmed the feeling that I had while driving to the hospital.

As the door to the room was opened, I saw both my wife and the babysitter seated and crying. Upon entering the room, my wife reached for my hand as the babysitter rose from her chair to hug me saying, "I'm so sorry, I'm so sorry Wayne" repeatedly. While waiting to find out what was occurring in the emergency room, the babysitter informed me that somehow a dime found it's way into the playpen and Ashley had stuck the dime into her mouth. In a matter of moments, Ashley had choked on the dime. The babysitter was only out of the room for moments. When she returned, she recognized the blue lips, and immediately began infant CPR and called 911. The babysitter, her husband, and two children lived less than a mile from the nearest fire station, and when the call for help was broadcast over the net, a neighbor, who was also a fireman, heard the call on his scanner and rushed across the street to render assistance. After sweeping the mouth and retrieving the dime, both the fireman and the babysitter worked together performing CPR until the ambulance arrived.

We sat there waiting what seemed to be an eternity. As the women cried, I could feel the anger building inside me, not knowing what was going on, not having any control of the situation, and already feeling the sense of regret. Finally, a nurse came to the door and informed us that if we wanted to see our daughter, now would be the time to see her. As my wife and I walked down the hallway holding each other's hand, each step seemed to take our breath away as we approached the emergency room.

Entering the room, you could see a mass of doctors and nurses surrounding Ashley's small and fragile body. My wife immediately let go of my hand and attempted to approach Ashley with all the tubes and wires connected, as she approached she broke down in tears seeing our daughter in this state. I on the other hand, still in uniform acted as a soldier, and set forth a barrage of questions to the doctors, nurses, and the recorder as I stared at the monitors. Not receiving any response, I spoke again in a slightly more direct manner and received a quick response to each question I posed, to include my most frightening: how long was she without oxygen? They responded that she was placed on oxygen as soon as the ambulance arrived. Though not satisfied with this answer, I knew it was the best I was going to receive.

I walked over and stood beside my daughter, all the while looking at the monitors. Twenty-four, twenty-four was her pulse, my throat became dry, the feeling inside my chest felt as someone had just hit me with a bat. My wife told Ashley that we were right there next to her, and that she needed to come back to us. As we watched her, I could feel the eyes of the emergency room staff look at us with somber reserve. One of the doctors approached and said that they were about to give a fourth shot of atropine. If that didn't work, there was nothing else that they could do. The shot was administered, and suddenly her pulse jumped to 118....115...117...116...117, the ER staff quickly moved us aside and began frantically working on Ashley again. After 10 minutes and finally a stable pulse, we were told that Ashley would be moved to the intensive care unit (ICU) for further observation and to see if any response of brain activity was occurring.

For a little over a day and a half, we sat, watched, and waited as the compassionate ICU staff worked with Ashley. As we sat and waited, close friends and acquaintances were present to offer their moral support. Acquaintances whom I hardly knew from my new duty assignment went to the airport to pick up my mother who had flown down from Massachusetts to be by my side. They went to our house, and returned with clothes so I could change out of my uniform and regularly brought food to us from the cafeteria. After a day and a half of waiting and watching tests being run again and again, and seeing my daughter underneath a heating lamp to help maintain her temperature, I had the consultation with the neurologist. We were informed that there was no brain activity and that she was brain dead.

The neurologist stated that we could either leave her on life support and that they would eventually pronounce her dead, or that I could make the call to pull the plug slightly earlier and not prolong the family's false sense of hope. Hearing this news, we were immediately on the phone with doctors and specialists from one of the best children's hospital in Boston to see if we could have her transferred there to see if there was anything they could provide. The repeated response was that there was nothing else that could be done. I informed the neurologist that I would consent to moving my daughter off life support. Shortly after the neurologist left, a member of the hospital staff approached us and asked if we had considered donating Ashley's organs to help other babies who might be in critical condition. At first, we were appalled because we were just digesting the fact that she was gone. The nurse, realizing the timing, spun on her heels and began walking away when we both replied, "Yes".

The next morning family and friends had the opportunity to say goodbye to Ashley before leaving the hospital. After everyone left, I went into the hospital room one last time to say goodbye to my daughter. The mixed emotions that I experienced vacillated between helplessness, anger, feeling like a failure, guilt, and wondering why this had to happen. As I was sitting beside the hospital bed holding her hand, a doctor arrived and informed me that it was time. As I held her hand, the doctor removed Ashley off life support and allowed me to remain with her for what I thought may have been minutes, but was evidently an hour or two. When the hospital staff came to help me from the room, I was lost; what do I do now?

The staff told me that they needed to know what funeral parlor would be handling the arrangements; I looked at them quizzically and told them I had no idea. The nurse came back and handed me a telephone book and told me I should find someone to call that could help organize the funeral arrangements and the cremation. Never having gone through this before, I was lost at what to do and started thumbing my way though the telephone book feeling rather frustrated. I called the first funeral home I found, they made sense out of my disjointed conversation and handled everything for me so I would not have to deal with any of the details.

Details, details were everywhere it seemed, and trying to make heads or tails of any situation under these circumstances began to overwhelm me. I had to deal with people, from my wife, who was going through her own emotional and grieving time, to extended family and friends, who wanted to show their support and be there for us. Although this can be of great assistance, at the time when trying to cope with the rollercoaster of emotions, this is not what I wanted or capable of handling.

Family had flown in while we were at the hospital and remained there until they said goodbye to Ashley. As I was on the All American Expressway headed home, my thoughts changed from thinking of my daughter, to where our family was going to stay. What were they going to eat? Why do they have to be here? Most importantly, why can't I just be alone? When I finally arrived at the house, our family was meandering around the living room and kitchen with plates of food. As I walked into the kitchen, I found the refrigerator and countertops filled with dishes of pre-made food that were brought to our house by some of the men with whom I had recently started working. Unbeknownst to me at the time and not discovered until a few months later, these men belonged to a fraternity that I had only read about growing up in New England. Although always fascinated by them, I had never taken any steps to join the Free and Accepted Masons. The question of what to do about feeding my family was answered by this simple gesture as both my mind and my spirit didn't care about anything that was going on. Various other details seemed to develop, but so much became a blur. At the time, I felt as if I couldn't focus and a perpetual cycle began to develop where I felt out of control.

I was, and still am, a man who is accustomed to being in control. This had been my train of thought throughout childhood, and was more evident the longer I served in the military. Unfortunately, this event was not supposed to occur. This was not the normal order that was to occur in life. So for a man who was used to being in control, I found out quickly that my life was spinning out of control and there was nothing I could do to change it.

When I walked into the emergency room and started questioning what actions were taking place with my daughter, I always believed that this was just because I was concerned and wanted to see that she was being cared for. It wasn't until years later, when I was sharing my experience with someone else, that I realized part of what I was doing was attempting to take control of the situation. When that didn't occur, I was adrift in unfamiliar territory.

Many of us are used to being in charge either at home, at work, or in other social activities in which we participate. When we suffer a loss, especially that of a child, we begin to develop and feel a sense of failure as we were unable to control the situation and circumstances revolving around the loss. That loss of control begins to trigger various emotions and a cycle that is challenging for us to deal and more importantly accept so we can begin our personal journey through the grieving process.

Chapter Two

Stages

After my daughter died, I was lost and wasn't sure what to do. This was the first time I had experienced something like this and was not prepared at all. Neither faith nor friends could comfort me. In fact, I began questioning my faith and didn't have the desire to speak with anyone. I became tired and angry (not frustrated, but angry) hearing the following:

- "I'm sorry"
- "I'm sorry for your loss"
- "I couldn't imagine what you're going through"
- "Is there anything I can do for you?"
- "God has his reasons for everything. God has a plan, or she is in Heaven now"

Each of these and many more were met with an answer underneath my breath.

- You're sorry, why are you sorry? You didn't lose your child.
- You're sorry for my loss, that's right it's my loss and you don't understand. You didn't lose your child.
- You can't imagine what I am going through. Of course not you didn't lose your child.
- Is there anything you can do, yes, either shut up and leave me alone, or bring my daughter back to me.

- I don't care what the reason is. I don't care that he has a plan. I don't care that she is in Heaven; I want my daughter. This is unfair.

I know each person who said this (family, friends, acquaintances, and hospital staff) had the best intentions, but I was upset. My wife was overcome with grief, upset, and slowly venturing toward depression. After going to the bookstore, we purchased some books on grief and how to overcome it. After thumbing through multiple books, I found myself growing angrier by the minute. These books shared the typical grief cycle, and what one should do to overcome their grief. But none of these books spoke about what *I* was feeling.

My trip to seek counseling...

My wife decided to go to grief counseling, and after a session or two she asked if I would go with her. As I was in the military and held a Top Secret security clearance, I knew that one of the questions on the security questionnaire asked if the person filling out the questionnaire had ever had psychological help or counseling (This has changed over the years, especially with the amount of people suffering from Post Traumatic Stress Disorder that have been identified since Operation Enduring Freedom and Operation Iraqi Freedom). Since this was a question at the time, I was reluctant to go to counseling, but as anger- no, rage- filled me, I felt that maybe this would be the best option for me. We went to the office and the counselor greeted us in a somber manner, as if she had been through the whole ordeal with us. And although I was offish, she was pleasant and told me it would be okay for me to sit there and would not even need to speak during that session. As the session went on, the counselor explained the grieving process and how we would work together to overcome this grief, just as the books described. I sat there feeling my pulse quicken, my ears and face becoming hot and turning red. The counselor asked if I had something I wanted to share. Share-yes, I wanted to share that this was not the way I was feeling. That for a professional the counselor was an idiot. Instead, I asked one question. "Have you lost your child?" The response was "No"; the counselor hadn't even had a child yet. At that point, I stood up and walked out of the office and to the car seething. My wife finally joined me and began telling me that I should give her a chance, and that if not her, we could find another counselor to meet with. My answer was simple, with probably some explicit language before and after the emphatic "*NO*". While this was not for me, I do understand that for some the counselor may be able to offer the appropriate assistance to assist one work through their grief. For me, I felt more alone, and began questioning if something was wrong with me and the way I was feeling.

Coping after the counselor...

Everyone will agree that grief is handled differently. What I had was discovering is that we are expected to either hear or read about the grieving process and allow ourselves to conform to that specific model. Well, those options didn't suit me. So when I started writing this twelve years ago, its original purpose was a journal to vent without the feeling of being judged. I could express myself without having to feel as if I was under the microscope or worrying that I may offend someone by sharing something they didn't want to hear, as it may hurt their feelings despite their best of intentions.

The challenge I faced every time I would write something down was that I would become so upset I would walk away from writing or destroy it, only to find myself writing it again and again. Not many understand or can deal with the death of a child; I later realized that my writings or venting might be able to help others cope with their own feelings and understand they are not alone. These insights may even help family understand what thoughts may be going through a fathers' head.

You have to be kidding right...

Less than a year after my daughter died, the same military chaplain of the XVIIIth Airborne Corps, who visited me in the hospital, came to my place of work to ask for assistance in speaking with a father who had recently lost a child. At that moment, I thought he had to be kidding. How could this man ask me to speak with another individual who had just lost a child since I was still trying to cope with my loss as well? Though I think my ears may have turned bright red, I don't think he realized that the anger building almost resulted in my losing composure and striking a military officer. He continued talking. I just stared at him blankly until he placed a piece of paper in my hand that had the name and number of this young junior enlisted soldier. I remember the Chaplain told me the young soldier had lost his son two days earlier from Sudden Infant Death Syndrome (SIDS), and that the Chaplain still felt uncomfortable speaking to a parent who had lost a child. Reluctantly, I accepted the task and went to the soldiers home to provide some sort of support from the military.

I knew what he didn't want to hear; I knew what he was feeling, and I knew he didn't need someone telling him how he should feel. Instead, I shared with him that it was okay to be angry; he had the right to be upset. When the time came that he needed to vent his frustration and anger, he could give me a call, and I would listen and not say a word. Two months went by before I received a call asking if we could meet somewhere to talk. We met at a local fast food restaurant on Fort Bragg, and he shared how upset he was that everyone kept telling him things would be all right. He was upset that his parents didn't understand what he was going through, and that his wife couldn't understand why he was angry. He vented for almost two hours and, as promised, I never spoke a word. He finally asked me one question, "Is it natural for me to be angry?" After I replied with a simple yes, he stood up and walked out.

A week passed and I received another phone call, this time not from the soldier, but from his wife. She told me that the Chaplain had given her my number and that she should call me for a better understanding of what her husband is feeling. Again, my initial feelings were anger. I am trying to deal with the death of my daughter and the Chaplain continues to hand off his work to me. I reluctantly agreed to meet her, and chose the very same, very public, fast food restaurant to speak with her.

When we met, she told me that she went out and bought books on grief and couldn't understand why when she tried to encouraged her husband to read them he would become angry and storm out of the house. She questioned why he didn't follow the grieving process like she was, and why he wouldn't attend any counseling or support groups. I shared with her what I was slowly discovering about myself as I reread my journal, that our grief process is different. Maybe because we were in the military, maybe because we were fathers, or maybe because we were men, but what he was feeling was natural and she needed to be patient and understanding as he worked through his personal grief cycle. Knowing that he was working through his grief was something that she had not realized, because his grief process was different than hers. I told her that it was all right for her husband to be angry, that he wasn't angry at her, but at himself and the situation. As she listened intently, I could see a calmness come across her face as I explained the cycle I was experiencing. She acknowledged that her husband was going through a similar cycle of emotions, and she was concerned because it wasn't found in any of her books on grief.

Four months later, the same young soldier came to see me once again. He explained that things between him and his wife were better and thanked me for taking the time to speak with her, since this helped her understand that he was dealing with grief in his own way. I was utterly amazed. I was able to help someone else, but I still hadn't accepted my daughter's death. In addition, my marriage was suffering because I felt I couldn't share what I was feeling with my wife.

What I came to realize was that I was experiencing a continuous cycle that further frustrated me, since I could not find a way to bring it to an end. For each person, the duration of the cycle is different. Sometimes a person can spend weeks in one stage and then move to another, or they can transition through the stages rather quickly finding constant frustration. It all depends on the individual,how they are feeling, and what message they feel others are telling them.

In the figure above, are the stages that I experienced during my personal grief cycle:

1. The sense of helplessness from not fulfilling your duty
2. Angry at everything all the time
3. Alone: desire to be left alone and not hear from others
4. Questioning: why; why did this happen
5. Return of the Anger: lack of communication and frustration begins to be exhibited

Often, one hears that some of the most stressful times in a person's life are getting married, getting divorced, buying a home, and losing a loved one. Since I have experienced all of those situations, I still feel losing a loved one is the worst. After speaking with the wife of the soldier, I dove into work so much that I was never at home. I didn't want to be home, since constant reminders of Ashley surrounded me. Never mind the fact that I didn't my wife to ask how I was doing, or if I was grieving, or if I could sit with her to talk through what she was feeling. I felt that speaking would just get me angry, since I didn't have any answers as to why this happened. In fact, I was still in shock and disbelief.

Though I knew that Ashley died, I still couldn't believe this had happened, and I began blaming myself. What could I have done differently? Maybe if we didn't move to North Carolina, maybe if we didn't need to have a babysitter, maybe if I didn't join the Army, maybe if we didn't have a child, or maybe God didn't want me to have a child? All of these thoughts went through my mind, and although they may have been irrational, I am sure some reading this book may have felt the same.

Depending on personal religious beliefs, some may become upset and wonder how could I think that God didn't want me to have a child. One may say I should leave everything in God's hands, as he is the Great Architect and has the blueprints for my life. Well, one thing I know is that any rational thought seemed to exhaust me during that time, so I continued in my mindset. Like many, I became angry with God questioning why. Only to have others tell me that I shouldn't question why, as this is all part of a master plan for me. In fact, not only was I beginning to become upset and angry with God, but I also lost myself and began questioned my faith. Though I heard the words these people were sharing, this still didn't help nor relieve the feelings or questions I had. What I slowly began to accept rational or not, was that maybe I wasn't meant to have a child.

Prior to Ashley being born, my wife had a miscarriage, and we had worked our way through that situation. But after Ashley died, I didn't think I could work my way through until I accepted that maybe I had done something that God didn't like, and this was my punishment-not having a child. Growing up, I was raised in a Christian household and my mother had hopes that one day I would become a preacher. I thought that maybe this was punishment for joining the Army and not becoming a preacher. This feeling lasted for years, and even after a divorce and remarriage, I refused to have another child. Although this may have been unfair to my new wife, Christy, and selfish on my part, I didn't think I could mentally handle the possibility of losing another child. I couldn't bear to think of going through that stage of helplessness again.

Chapter Three

Helplessness

Helpless, I can't imagine another word that could explain what I felt when my daughter was in the hospital, and I had to sit there not able to do a thing. Helpless, no other word could sum up the feeling when I was told my daughter was brain dead, and I would need to shut off life support or wait until the doctor turned it off. Helpless- the feeling that I had failed as a father and a protector. When I was sitting in the hospital room, I was lost. I didn't have anything to do; I couldn't do anything but sit and wait and be at the mercy of time, doctors, and God. For a person who is used to taking charge, being in charge, or always having a plan, this experience made me feel as if I were a child who couldn't do anything on my own. I felt as if I was incapacitated and could only watch everything go on around me. Yes, I could ask questions to the medical staff, but that provided little comfort, as the answers were the same. Finally the staff just stopped coming to the waiting room to provide any answers.

Why does it consume us…

The reasons previously mentioned, along with so many other explanations, is the reason why helplessness begins the cycle that slowly consumes us. Why is it, that the feeling of helplessness consumes us: it is the attack that the feeling has on our own pride and ego. Whether you were raised in a nuclear family, a single parent home, or were without parents, societal norms, television, and examples throughout history show boys that when you become a man. There are certain expectations and obligations that are followed as you progress towards adulthood. The challenge many men face is that model is not reality; it is only a template that one uses to help define their maturity, character, and handling of situations as they age.

Since the loss of a child is so traumatic and taboo of a subject, most men have no idea how to handle this situation. Sometimes a man will go to other men, such as their father, their close friends, or a religious figure in order to seek advice as to how to handle the situation. Yet other times, a man will find that there is no one else to which he can turn, and will then have to deal with and solve the situation on his own, creating that feeling of helplessness.

Classic manology...

From the earliest of times, we are taught in a classic sense that man is the protector and provider of his family. Though this may not always be true, the societal norm remains a constant, and reminds the male that he is ultimately responsible for protecting his family. A quick journey though history displays this quite well. From looking back to the depictions of the cave men, one can see that the males served as the protector of the tribe and were responsible for their family's well-being and safety. Continue to move along through history and see example upon example of how this concept is applied throughout time and the world.

A man can almost think that based upon history and television, we see the protector role as an expected part of who we are or whom we are supposed to be. Multiply that feeling by a job where you are a protector (military, police, fire, etc.); the sense of protection you would expect to provide to your family is even further intensified. Growing up, I looked at this model as an example. This could have been because my mother and father divorced at an early age and I to others and television to help provide a reference on how to act. I was taught to find various elements of men in history and in my life that I wanted to emulate and use that to help guide me as I grew into manhood.

Though that may sound great and inspirational for some, one subject was never covered…how to deal with the death of my daughter. I felt I had nowhere to turn, and though I spoke to my mother and my father, there were no answers as to what I should do in this situation. I was alone. However, worse then being alone in this situation was the fact that I felt as if I had failed as a father, a husband, and a man.

Sense of failure…

Growing up I was taught that through hard work, one can accomplish anything. I believed this philosophy well into my thirties. It wasn't until I read other books that I realized hard work alone is not what will grant you success, but it will help you accomplish many things. In fact, until the death of my daughter (when I was 25 years old), I could only think of two circumstances that could be true set back in my life. Some may not think that is much, but after the childhood I had and the struggle to make something out of myself, I thought I had beaten the odds...until now.

When Ashley died, I felt as if I had failed. I failed to protect her; I failed to keep her safe, and I failed to fulfill my responsibility as a father. As I sat in the hospital room, I replayed the previous evening. I replayed the events of that morning, and I wished that there were something I could have done to change the outcome. I wished that I never came to North Carolina. I wished that my wife didn't need to work. I wished that we didn't need a babysitter. I wished so much, but only to face the fact that no matter what, I had failed.

After growing up in a divorced home, I was determined I would always be there for my children; I would be there to share in their highs and their lows. I was determined that if I promised something, I would fulfill that promise and not let my children face the same disappointment I experienced growing up. I had made a promise, and it was a promise that I didn't fulfill. I promised to take care of my daughter, and in that that I failed.

Not only did I fail her, but I failed my wife as well. She counted on me to keep the family safe; she counted on me as the protector to not let anything happen to her or our daughter. How could I look at her, or any other member of our family, after I had failed all of them by letting something happen to my daughter? I had let them all down. Although my wife never blamed me, every time I looked at her I felt as if she were blaming me for allowing this to happen to our daughter. I felt that she was disappointed because I didn't fulfill my responsibility in protecting my daughter. Even worse, was when she wanted to talk about grief and how she was feeling. I would take this as a personal attack on my failure rather than her way of coping with the situation. Unfortunately, these same internal thoughts further created a void between us, as I never shared how I felt.

Years would go by, a divorce, and a new marriage before I learned that I needed to share how I felt about certain things. Still today, I am reluctant to share all of my feelings with Christy. This sense of failure as the protector is hard to deal with and begins to eat away at us daily. In my case, I didn't want to make additional decisions, even though I was depended upon to make them. I felt that I wasn't worthy and didn't want the responsibility, since I couldn't keep my daughter safe. A continuous pattern begins in which you have no desire to do anything or make any decisions because you failed. After speaking to a friend years later, who happened to be a psychologist, he attributed the fact that the feeling of failure is one of the more challenging feelings to overcome, especially if you don't have a second chance to rectify the situation. When a father loses a child, you don't have that chance with that child again; there is no rewind.

Blame game...

Although I knew that my wife and family were not blaming me for Ashley's death, I couldn't help but feel that they were. Feelings are a hard thing to change. People can change your opinions, but feelings are your own and not something that can be changed by someone simply stating a few kind words, showing empathy, or trying to understand your situation. I felt I was to blame, and that everyone around me was blaming me for what had happened to Ashley.

Because of the circumstances around Ashley's death, the police responded to question the babysitter, my wife, and myself regarding how Ashley died. Although this was a simple case, and the questions they asked all pertained to the babysitter, I felt as if they were blaming me. I felt that even the police were blaming me and thinking how could I be such a horrible father to have my daughter with a babysitter. I realize now that this was probably not the case, but at the time, my sense of failure and of helplessness made me feel as if I were being blaming for my daughter's death.

At the same time, I could see my wife was blaming herself as well. She was blaming herself for dropping our daughter off at the babysitter, for having to go to work, and for allowing this to happen even though it was outside her control. She probably felt as if I were blaming her for our daughter's death, and felt I would continue to blame her and never forgive her. She heard me tell her while at the hospital, and afterwards, that she wasn't to blame. However, as I stated previously, a feeling won't be changed with a few kind words. While she was going through her grieving process, I would attempt to console her with the stale words, that she was not to blame. Yet, I think because of the coldness of the words, she may have thought and felt otherwise. I was little help since I still had to accept my daughter's death as well.

Next in line to blame of course would be the babysitter. Yet, contrary to her thoughts, I didn't blame her at all. In fact, when questioned by the police, they were surprised how much confidence I had that she had taken all the appropriate measures to protect Ashley. I had known the babysitter and her family since our previous assignment in Hawaii. Her husband had worked in the same platoon as me, and would visit with us every time they would come down to Honolulu from Schofield Barracks. When her husband received orders to Ft Bragg, they came to visit us shortly after their arrival. When my wife began working in Fayetteville, this woman was quick to volunteer to babysit, as she always wanted a little girl to spoil.

Spoil Ashley they did, both her and her two sons would wear Ashley out by playing with her throughout the day. They would buy outfits for her when they were out shopping on their own, and they would always want to make sure she was invited to participate in any activity they were doing. I can't even begin to tell how many times we would send Ashley over with two or three changes of clothes, only to have her come home with five or six. When her sons found out they were going for a hayride, they wanted to make sure Ashley could come as well. The babysitter treated Ashley like the daughter she never had.

When I heard what had happened, I couldn't believe it. I knew how careful she was with Ashley; I knew that she would always take care of her. I couldn't blame her; I still felt that I was the one ultimately responsible. Months after Ashley's death, she and her husband stopped speaking to me. Not because I blamed them, but because she blamed herself and couldn't face seeing us as a constant reminder of that horrendous day. I find this unfortunate, as tragedy has continued to plague her life; her husband was later killed in action while serving in Iraq. To this day, I wish I could have been there for her as she was there for us when we lost Ashley.

Blaming family...

In my situation, my wife was not to blame, and I didn't blame the babysitter. For others, there may be someone out there that they blame for the death of their child. This is not something that is easy to overcome. In fact, it causes further anger and frustration as the feeling of helplessness continues to gnaw away at you. Depending on the circumstances and who the individual is, you feel helpless in resolving the anger you may have towards the individual.

If the person is your spouse, the option of divorce exists, but may not be one you want to consider. If the individual is another child of yours, you find yourself in a truly difficult situation. You must deal with your feelings towards the child you blame. I'm not going to say not to blame someone else. In fact, I think you do more harm to yourself when you try not to blame a person when you feel they are responsible. What I will say is that you need to realize this is something you will have to come to terms with and balance out yourself. This is an easy task, and there are no simple solutions or answers on how to resolve this feeling. What you do need to acknowledge is that you may feel slightly helpless and that it is natural.

Blaming others...

Should you find there is another person to blame, you will most likely be frustrated as you feel you cannot take any direct action to resolve this feeling. If the other individual died at the same time as your child or shortly thereafter, both anger and helplessness intensifies. Knowing that there was another person to blame, but not being able to hold them accountable for their actions creates that helpless void with no solution in sight. Yes, years and years can pass, but the desire to have a person to look at and blame remains. Should the person to blame be around, the blame never feels as if it does justice to the loss of your child. Knowing that another person may be held accountable presents some sort of slight gratification, but never fills the void of the lost child. The feeling of helplessness continues to resonate inside you, festering anger at the situation. The grieving process can take longer and seem like it will never end.

After Ashley died, and for years afterward, I blamed someone else. I searched for a reason why my daughter died and wanted to know who was truly accountable. I eventually satisfied this search for answers and settled on one individual who I blamed for my daughters death: The boy who threw the rubber coin purse into the room the previous evening. I was angry. I blamed him, and settled this in my mind that he was the reason my daughter was gone. Do I still blame him today? I would probably lie to you if I said I didn't. Do I wish ill will on him or any harm to come to him? Not any more.

While talking with others, I realized that this is part of the process. Determining blame and if there is someone accountable is part of the process each and every person who loses someone unexpectedly ends up committing time and effort. Is this right to find someone to blame? Well, I am not one to judge as this is between you and your conscious, but I do feel this is part of your grieving process and a step to moving forward ever so slightly.

Helplessness to answerless in the waiting room...

The first onslaught of questions came when I was at the hospital, with family, friends, and colleagues alike all surrounding me asking what they could do to help. The answer was simple at that time, bring Ashley back to me; let her wake up and breath on her own. Of course, that didn't happen, and they couldn't bring her back to me. These individuals all wanted to show their support and willingness to help, but at that time, I didn't know what I needed help with. I knew that I felt lost and alone. I knew that I didn't want people around, yet I didn't want to be sitting there by myself. I didn't want people to speak to me. I didn't want them to offer their sympathy, their support, or say that they were there to help me. I didn't know what I wanted, or even if I wanted them around at all.

Sitting in the waiting room, I watched as these family and friends sat with my wife and spoke to her in their attempts to console and comfort her. Quietly, I resented that; I resented the fact that someone was able to say something that brought some sort of comfort to my wife. I wondered how she could be comforted when our daughter was still lying in the hospital crib on life support. My resent would turn instantly to anger, and I would have to hunch over in my chair and put my head down so others would not see the anger on my face. As new people would come in, or others would return, all the same questions would be asked again.

- Are there any new developments?
- How is she?
- How are you holding up?
- Is there anything I can do for you?
- Is there anything I can get you?
- Do you need something to eat?

The answers were always an outwardly polite "No", but inwardly the comments were flying. The anger that these questions brought about would continue to fester for hours on end. People would leave, and I would still be angry at them. They would stay and sleep in the waiting room; I would be mad that not only did they ask those questions but sleep as well. What could I say? What could they do to help? I just didn't know.

Still answerless...

After Ashley died, the questions not only continued, but also seemed to increase.

- Is there anything I can do for you?
- How are you holding up?
- What can I do to help?
- Are you coping all right?
- Are you grieving?
- Why won't you speak with me?

These questions, along with many more, began to inundate me on a daily basis, and unfortunately I had no real answer to provide. The day Ashley was taken off life support, I had to speak with the funeral home. They asked a slew of questions, which I tried to answer the best I could but seemed to no avail. I placed a nurse on the phone with the funeral parlor who gave them all of the information they needed in order to cremate her.

When I arrived at home, after what seemed to be the longest drive I had ever taken, friends and family asked me if we were going to have a wake. Were going to have a funeral there in North Carolina, or if we would hold one back in New England? I felt like a boxer who had just gone the distance in a ring with no decision being made, and I felt exhausted. After a few minutes in the house with all of the friends and family, I walked into Ashley's bedroom and just stood there.

My mother came up beside me, hugged me, and told me she was sorry. I didn't reply; I didn't want anyone around me. I just wanted to be alone. She stood there for a while and asked if I needed anything, again I remained silent and she finally left. Shortly afterwards my wife approached and stood by my side and asked if I was alright. I remained silent and she left. How could I be all right I wondered, I just had to take my daughter off life support, I just had to watch my daughter die in front of me, I just held my daughters lifeless body. The question seemed unreasonable, and I knew that this would not be the first time, or the last that this question would be posed.

The questions continued over time, months in fact, and then all of a sudden the questions came to an end. This could have been because I continued to turn away the offers of assistance. Maybe the negative response finally informed people that I didn't want to speak about this. Maybe they thought that I had come to terms, grieved for my daughter, and moved on. Whatever the case, the questions finally stopped.

Still helpless...

Although the questions stopped, I still felt helpless, because I couldn't find the answers that I needed. I still couldn't come to terms with Ashley's death, and I wasn't sure if I could speak with my wife or anyone else about how I felt. When the Chaplain asked that I speak with the young family who lost their child to SIDS, I felt that I couldn't speak with them, since I was still trying to come to terms with Ashley's death. I still felt that I had failed as a father and as a protector of my family.

I later learned the painful truth; this feeling of helplessness was part of a cycle that I was going to go through multiple times and at different stages of my life as I continued to work through my personal grief cycle. This isn't meant to scare you, but to understand that it doesn't just happen once and then goes away. This feeling continues and the answers you may have developed the first or second time, may not always work the next time. When the feeling hits again, I can't say if it is better or worse than the first time you go through it; but I can say that it still hurts just as much if you are not prepared for it. For me, the feeling of being helpless and a failure as a father began to tear me apart so much that my mind eventually reached the unthinkable.

Depression by a different name...

This feeling of helplessness was a perpetual cycle that I didn't want to go through again and again. Like many who have lost someone they care about, they venture into a state of emptiness (some may call depression). I don't include the state of depression into my grief cycle, as I think that many of the categories spoken in this book could all be listed as a part of depression. Additionally, I didn't like someone telling me that I was going to be depressed because my daughter died, because I didn't feel depressed, I felt helpless, angry, lonely, inquisitive, and angry again. Depressed... not so much. I just didn't want someone (a counselor or psychologist) telling me his or her opinion of what was wrong with me. I knew what was wrong with me; I had lost my daughter.

My new friend...

During this incessant cycle of helplessness, I found a new friend that would help me (or so I thought) get past feeling helpless and a failure...alcohol. I came home one night, my wife wasn't home and I stared at a little red doll that my daughter had. I started remembering when she received it at Christmas, and how we played hide and seek with the doll. When the doll made noise she would look around and start crawling in the direction of the noise she had heard. I held the doll and pushed it, the noise went off, and I started crying. I walked over to a cupboard and pulled down a bottle of Irish whiskey, a glass, and I started drinking. After consuming ¾ of the bottle, I went to sleep.

The next day feeling slightly groggy, I managed to go to work and participate in the morning physical exercise training that was being conducted. That day, thoughts of failing as a father and a husband reared again, and I just wanted them to go away. That night I ended up having to work late, and by the time I came home my wife was already in bed asleep. Still having the same feeling, I reached in the cupboard and found the bottle again, but with only a ¼ remaining I felt unresolved. After work the next day, I stopped off at the Class Six (military version of a package store or place that sells alcohol) and purchased a bottle of whiskey.

Unfortunately, these only lasted two days, and I began to get angry once again as it seemed my new friend was letting me down. (Unfortunately, I would return to this friend many times over the next two years in an effort to ease my pain.) My thoughts of feeling helpless, embarrassed, ashamed, and a failure resulted in a feeling of being empty or dead inside. Frustrated that I didn't want to do anything or be around anyone, I felt as if there was nothing that would bring any life back to me. I just wanted all of this to end; I wanted the pain to go away.

An alternate "permanent" solution...

As I previously mentioned, this is a cycle and one that you have to be prepared for or at least aware of before the cycle takes its toll on you. After going through my short stage of alcohol dependency, the next time I felt helpless I immediately went to the anger stage and loneliness again. A short while later I was back to the helpless stage again. I was furious the feelings were reoccurring. I was upset that I couldn't find a solution to help me, but I was able to help someone else. That feeling of emptiness and feeling dead inside increased my desire to end the pain once and for all.

During this time that I can vividly remember being at work and as I was transitioning back and forth from being angry to feeling helpless, the thought of suicide crossed my mind. Not just the idea of suicide, but going home pulling my .45 caliber pistol out of the nightstand drawer, walking into my daughters room, sitting down in the rocking chair in the room and swallowing a bullet. I felt as if I were two people standing in the middle of the road; one looking at the other in disbelief that these thoughts were going through my mind. The worst part was that I was actually considering this to be an option. When training for any activity, I had always believed that if you could picture yourself doing something then you could accomplish it. But this was different; as I stood there I realized that I was picturing killing myself.

Now, I was raised that suicide wasn't the answer and that this was a cowardly thing that someone could do. In the military, I was taught that if you happened to have the thoughts of suicide and shared this, your clearance would be removed, you would be placed on suicide watch, and would be sent to mental health professionals to be examined. This is the first time that I have shared with anyone that these thoughts had crossed my mind. The reason for this is that if I had these thoughts, there are others out there who may have this passing thought as well. As I am writing this now, one can only surmise that I elected not to take my life nor did I even attempt it. Instead, I got angry. I was angry that I even thought of taking my own life. Yes, this would resolve the emptiness, but this wasn't what I wanted, taking my own life would not bring Ashley back to me.

Chapter Four

Anger

The first few chapters mentioned anger, and this entire chapter is committed to speaking about anger. The big difference in my discussion about anger is that not only do I accept that I was angry, I embraced this feeling. I can't begin to tell you how many books I have picked up speaking about grief that I have literally thrown back on the bookshelf, thrown across the room, ripped up, or tossed into the garbage all because they tell me how I shouldn't feel angry. Any child will tell you that if their toy is taken away or destroyed, they are angry. Heck you can see it on their face that they are livid. So how dare someone, who has not walked in your shoes or mine, have the audacity to say we shouldn't be angry. I was fed up with hearing counselors, friends, colleagues, and family tell me I shouldn't be upset any more. I was angry and at a whole variety of different things.

Listed below are some of the reasons I was angry:

- Everything and everyone
- For being helpless
- For feeling like a failure
- That I couldn't protect my daughter
- Angry that people kept saying they were sorry
- Angry that people just didn't understand
- That people wouldn't leave me alone
- That other people had children
- And angry that people weren't responsible parents or took their children for granted

I'm sure all of us have felt some of these same feelings and probably more as we reach the anger stage in our grief cycle.

What I want to share that is different from others opinions; you have the right to be angry. Don't try to avoid being angry. Accept the fact that you are angry and tell others to accept that you are angry as well.

Angry at everything and everyone...

After Ashley died, I seemed to be always angry. Especially during the first few months, everything seemed to get me upset. I was angry with the babysitter for having watched two other children the evening prior to Ashley's accident. I was especially angry with the child who had one of those rubber coin purses and threw the coin purse into the room where Ashley's playpen was kept. Why did that child have to be so misbehaved? Why did someone have to invent that stupid rubber coin purse?

The more I thought about the circumstances of the situation, the more I seemed to become angry and want to lash out at somebody or something. Every time I saw a doctor or a nurse walk by, I became upset because I wanted new news; I wanted to hear that Ashley started breathing on her own. The fact that I couldn't do anything but sit in the waiting room and wait further increased the frustration that I was having. I was not in control, I didn't have any say over this situation, and although I knew that I couldn't control anything I still became angry. I wanted to have some sort of say, I wanted to have some miniscule amount of control. Instead, I felt helpless.

Anger that we were so helpless...

Helpless again? Wasn't there just an entire chapter about helplessness? Yes, and as you read through that chapter you probably could sense the undertone of being upset and angry. I wanted to do something, I am a man of action, and I felt as if there just had to be something that I could do. While sitting there in the hospital waiting room the anger continued to fester inside of me, as there was nothing I could do. I was at the mercy of doctors and nurses, whom not only did I not know, but felt as if they were not taking every necessary step to take care of my daughter. Looking back, this wasn't the case and I have to give credit to all of the doctors and nurses who worked with my daughter, especially for having to put up with me. At the time, I felt as if they were only doing the minimal that could be done for my daughter, and every opportunity I had I questioned (alright, maybe it was more like grilled or interrogated) them regarding what was happening and what treatment they were conducting on Ashley. During my time at the hospital, I know I became argumentative at least twice (although I am sure it may have been more) with the doctors and nurses. I felt as if I had to do something; there had to be some type of action I could take.

With my mother's assistance through her connections to a children's' hospital back in Massachusetts, I had called to see if there was anyway that I could have Ashley transported to that hospital. The doctor on the phone asked to speak to the doctor treating Ashley, and after a short period of time I was handed back the phone. The response I received was not what I wanted to hear. I was told that transporting Ashley to Massachusetts was not a viable option as she was too unstable. The doctor on the other end of the phone attempted to assure me that the doctors in Fayetteville were doing everything they could and I should feel fortunate that she was still with us at that point. Of course, my natural reaction took over. He had to be wrong, he couldn't be right, there had to be another option. We were fortunate that she was lying in the intensive care unit not breathing on her own. Hearing this I became angry, angry with myself, my mother, the doctor in Massachusetts, and at the doctors here. There had to be something I could do, I couldn't just sit idly by.

If you happen to be reading this with the hopes of understanding what a loved one is going through, especially one who is used to being in charge or having control of situations, then understand this experience may be one of the worst experiences he or she will ever come across in their lives. Often this individual has had some sort of control of their destiny, or from experience or position they are used to being the individual who is in charge at home, work, or other activities in life. Although this could be tied to the sense of feeling helpless, I believe this conversation fits best here as the feeling of helplessness quickly changes to anger of not having control over the situation.

What do you do if you want to help? Simply stated-nothing. Now others (clergy, counselors, or others with doctorate degrees) may disagree with me completely, and that is fine. What I will share is that I didn't want to hear the kind word. I didn't want a hand on the shoulder, or even a hug. What I wanted was to be given my space. What I wanted was to hit someone or something. Would this change anything, not at all, but a small portion of me would feel slightly better.

Now, not all people may be going through this, but what you may find is if you have a loved one who may have been described above, they may be feeling this way. They don't want to talk, and when they do it seems as if they want to argue or if they are so volatile they will explode at any moment. This is *normal*; this is how some people feel they have to handle this type of situation. This is how they handle the feeling of being helpless.

Anger that we are a failure...

When I was a young teenager, I was encouraged to take Spanish for my foreign language credit in high school. Much to my dismay, I found that Spanish was a tad bit more challenging than I had first anticipated. No matter how hard I studied, or requested additional assignments, I ended up failing my first quarter. When I would come home, I would immediately go to my canvas punching bag and hit the bag for a couple of hours until my hands were bloody.

Did this solve anything? Not at all, I still had an F, but now I had a F and bloody hands.

That was the first time that I could ever recall that I had failed at something. I hated the feeling. Failure was something that I never wanted to accept, I had been told so many times growing up that I would fail or that I wouldn't amount to anything because of my family and economic situation. So, for me, this failure was hard to accept and I felt that I needed to punish myself for failing. Now, although that grade seemed devastating to me, that was nothing compared to the feeling I was having when I lost Ashley.

Some say that we are our own worst critics and when we lose a child, we begin to critique every aspect of our parenting ability.

As I write this book, my wife Christy will occasionally read over what I have written. She feels that I am to hard on myself and that I do not capture the true person I am. Though I acknowledge that she might be right, I also acknowledge that the feeling of being a failure is something extremely difficult to overcome. Previously, I mentioned how I felt when Ashley died that I had failed in my role, in my responsibility as a father. I felt that as others looked at me, they too were judging how I failed my daughter and was unable to be that responsible parent.

Never had I imagined that I would ever be in this situation. Never could I imagine feeling that I had not only let my daughter down, but I let down everyone who knew us as well. My body felt like it had imploded. I couldn't find any thoughts that seemed to comfort me. But comfort wasn't what I wanted; this wasn't what I thought I needed. Instead, I wanted to regress to years ago when I lashed out at that punching bag I had bloodied my hands against. I felt like I wanted to hit the walls in the hospital, and that I wanted to punish myself for not being there for Ashley.

During my personal grief cycle, punishing myself is exactly what I ended up doing. Not by punching the walls of the hospital, or the walls of our home, but by drinking. Drinking was an escape to provide some other feeling besides the helplessness, anger and loneliness that I was experiencing. The constant thought of being a failure as a person continued to overshadow me.

As a result, I stopped speaking to my wife, which perpetuated the thought that I was a failure as a husband. I didn't bother speaking with the grief counselors or even listening to what they were saying. As a result, the feeling that I had failed in my role as a parent continued to fester. The buildup of anger and lack of communication continued to drive a wedge between my wife and I, and I looked for other avenues of escape from my self-criticism. So, in an effort to help alleviate these thoughts, I returned to my old friend and attempted to drink my thoughts away.

My drinking would occur off and on, not really because of how I felt, but because of how I would think about myself.

Ashley died in January 1999 and my heavy bouts of drinking would continue until February 2001. Two years seems like such a short time, but when you are attempting to punish yourself, time and everything else seems so irrelevant.

What didn't seem irrelevant to me were my military duties. I spent more time at work than I did at home. I was successful in my position, and, though I was still hung over some days, I could still perform our physical training with little to no effort.

This was extremely fortunate for me as I was often able to disguise the alcohol seeping out of my pores and sober up prior to my other official duties. I think that knowing I could still perform my job was one of the reasons that I buried myself at work.

As I have spoken to other bereaved men, I have found that because they have no desire to be at home, they too often find refuge at work. For some, they didn't want to be at home with the constant reminder of their child. For others, they didn't want to be around their grieving spouse. While some found work to be a refuge where they could become so occupied with work that they wouldn't think of their loss until they were ready to leave for the day.

Some of us need to have a drive, something that keeps us going on a daily basis. When we feel or think that we are a failure, we often lose our motivation, our internal drive that we need to keep us afloat physically, emotionally and mentally. Some professionals, and even family members, may say that diving into work is completely wrong; that you are running away from your problems. What I would share is that although you may not want to confront those feelings, finding something that lessens the feeling of failure is something that we need in order to continue.

Unfortunately, because we often shut others out, they cannot discover that this is part of how some of us tend to deal with grief. I wouldn't say we are running away, I would say we are trying to adjust our own psyche and prove to ourselves that we are not a failure. Finding a way to accept that you are not a failure is just another step in coming to terms and dealing with your own grief cycle.

Anger that we couldn't protect...

This next point goes hand-in-hand with the previous thought of being a failure, but with a slight variation.

When Ashley was in the emergency room, I felt guilty that I couldn't protect her from being hurt. After she was moved to the intensive care unit, I felt angry that I hadn't been able to protect her and I was to blame for her being in the situation that we found ourselves. The longer I sat in the waiting room, the more I began to feel that I had failed to protect my little girl, and I had let my family down.

Anyone who watches television or movies will tell you on the screen the parental figure, be it a caveman or an alien, should conquer all odds to protect their children. History has shown that leaders have gone to war to protect their families; human nature expects us to protect our children... Always.

With just a quick glance at the news or a search on the internet, one can find articles speaking about how a parent appeared to have superhuman strength or speed in an effort to rescue their child from harm. With examples like these, we begin to formulate ideas about how we are supposed to be the protectors of our children. We also begin to recognize that our friends, family, colleagues and share this idea.

Take a moment to think about how much advice you received after having your child. The topics were so varied from how to cover electric outlets to which diapers may leave a rash. From beginning to save immediately for college, to how to discipline your child without having them run all over you (or without having them taken away for giving them a smack on the hand when they attempted to touch the stove). The advice was everywhere, even when it was unwanted and unwarranted. But, of course, this was all in an effort to help you protect the newest edition to your family.

What happens when you feel as if you were unable to protect your child and the rest of your family from tragedy, you become angry. And for those who are reading this trying to understand why your loved one won't open up and is angry all the time, it's because they have the right to be angry. We are angry about the situation, the inability to protect our child. We are angry that we did not fulfill our responsibilities to society as the protector of our family. We are not the superhero that our child had thought of us to be, or that we had hoped they would have envisioned us.

As a military leader, I had always looked at the soldiers in my charge as my responsibility. My duty was to coach, mentor, lead and protect them from making foolish decisions. After successfully working with numerous soldiers and keeping them out of harm's way, I was excited that I would be able to do the exact same thing (with more emphasis) to my own flesh and blood. But, after Ashley died, how could I protect others if I couldn't protect her?

I began questioning my ability to fulfill my role as the protector. Could I protect my wife now? What if something happened? Would I have failed in my responsibility again?

I often became angry, wondering what I would do and how I would handle various situations. I didn't want to feel helpless or that I could not protect. I needed to find some way to fill this void and reclaim my protector status within myself. Because I was so angry, to the point of being volatile, I needed to find some outlet to release my anger.

My solution was to venture back to my youth and embrace fighting. Not so much as to picking a fight with anyone walking down the street, although there were times I did want to do that very thing. Instead, I chose to embrace martial arts as a constructive way to focus and release my anger.

Having participated in many various martial arts growing up and in my military career, I decided to participate in Judo as a means of relief. The location I found to study Judo taught striking, submissions and throws – all elements that appealed to my primal self. I enjoyed the feeling of throwing another person through the air, only to be met seconds later with me holding them down and working a submission, waiting to hear them give up or tap. I needed this outlet, not only to rebuild my confidence as a protector, but as the conduit to release my anger, especially since I still had quite a bit of it and it wasn't fading away.

Angry that people keep and kept saying they were sorry...

Earlier, I mentioned how just hearing the word "sorry" would make me see red. While waiting in the small room while Ashley was in the emergency room, the hospital counselor had said how sorry she was for us that Ashley was in such a grave condition.

Hearing that, I immediately became upset. Had this woman already given up my daughter, had she just told me that she was sorry and there was no hope for Ashley's recovery?

I was furious, but at the same time I just wanted to see what was being done and if Ashley was receiving every opportunity. When we eventually moved upstairs to the waiting room for the intensive care unit, family, friends, and coworkers slowly migrated into the room, all to say they were sorry. Each time I heard those words, I felt as if someone was hitting me in the crotch and giving up hope that Ashley would survive. I wasn't sure if I was feeling more devastated from hearing "sorry", or if the words made me angrier.

To remedy this, I found that I would spend quite a bit of time in the instead of the waiting room. That way I wouldn't have to face or deal with anyone that had just come in. Of course, when I made my way back to the waiting room, everyone wanted to tell me how sorry they were, and that they wished there was something they could do to help. I was just so tired of hearing people say that they were sorry, that the words became fake and insincere to me. Now I know these people were sincerely sorry that this happened to Ashley, but at that time in my life I didn't want to hear those words. It felt as if all hope had been lost.

After Ashley died, I was still surrounded by people who were determined to say they were sorry that Ashley died. Even after years have gone bye, when someone hears that I had lost a child the first word they usually say is "sorry". For years, I would be frustrated that people would say this. People who didn't even know my daughter or really know me.

In the early years, I would become upset and resort to my old mantra of why were they sorry: they hadn't lost a child, they hadn't lived through this tragic event, and they had no idea how this felt. Initially, I believe that those words were the initial trigger recalling the circumstances of that very day. The words would seem to stop me dead in my tracks and transport me back to the initial phone call; being moved to the side room off of the emergency room; feeling helpless, and acknowledging that there was nothing I could do and that my little girl was going to die.

I know that this was not what was meant when someone said they were sorry, but these were the hard memories that I had to face each time. I can't tell you exactly when, maybe it was after nine or ten years the words seemed easier to digest. After what seemed to be an eternity, what I have come to realize is that people have no idea what to say or how to react to this type of circumstance.

The idea of losing a child is so removed from a person, finding the words to show support or comfort just doesn't seem to exist. Today many grief support groups exist and although you may be opposed to joining one now, it is something to consider in the future (I'll talk about these and the associated anxiety in a later chapter).

Angry that people won't leave you alone...

How many times have you said out loud or internally to someone else that you just want them to leave you alone so you can deal with the death on your own terms? I know that I have wished the exact same thing on multiple occasions. Why can't people seem to understand that I don't need, or want their assistance or want to have them around me?

We all go through this stage. Whether you have lost a loved one or not, I am sure that many people can relate to this same feeling at some level or another. Have you ever had a person that just seems to get on your nerves, always hanging around your or in your close proximity? Adults and children alike all seem to experience this same feeling that the other person is always there, and in your face. For me, having someone always around who seemed as if they wanted to do something, say something, or give a look as if they were waiting for me to share something made my blood boil.

From my experience, a part of us wants to have people around, but another part wants to be left alone without any interaction. For me, I was angry that people wanted to be there to support me. I would get angry thinking that the only reason why they were there was because they felt guilty not knowing the right thing to do or say. Family and friends were around to help if we needed something, and although they understood I was upset, I don't think they realized that by being around they helped fuel the anger and frustration I was feeling. I wanted to escape. I wanted to escape to my own little area and not deal with people wanting to speak with me or be around me.

Although I felt that I wanted to be by myself, I probably would have done more damage if people weren't there. I found that although I couldn't escape physically all the time, I could escape mentally (I will speak about this when we explore the chapter on the Cave) and I did just that to remove myself from having to deal with people being around.

Angry that others exist...

This next section will probably be extremely controversial to some, in fact I am sure some would even criticize me for thinking what I am about to talk about, never mind the fact that I am going to place the thought in print.

Angry that others exist can be interpreted in so many different formats, but after I lost Ashley, I realized that I would become angry every time I saw another baby or toddler. I was angry at the sight of another baby; I was angry at people who had children. I wanted to be nowhere around them. Life just seemed after losing Ashley, and seeing a child only reminded me of her and that I couldn't have her beside me. Unfortunately, everywhere I went, I seemed to run into a small child. If I went to the grocery store, no matter the time (yes, even at midnight) there was a child in the shopping cart being pushed by one of his parents. When I went to a fast food restaurant, there were children in the establishment's playground. One would think that a breeding frenzy had. I can't begin to tell you how many times I left a shopping cart in a store and walked out; or how many times I ordered and paid for my food, but then left without it because I couldn't stand the sight of seeing a child.

Now, some of you may think this is or was extreme, but I can tell you now, that some of those individuals you love and care about so much feel the exact same way. They feel so angry every time they see another child or one close to the same age or characteristics of the one they lost that they can't even be in the same vicinity.

For some, the feeling is immediate; for others, this feeling is something that develops over a period of time. This could be a month, a year, or out of nowhere, five years later. I have spoken with some parents that have lost children and to this day they still choose to vacation at resorts where children are not welcome. They find this easier to accept then having to deal with feelings that they just may not be willing to accept.

For others, this feeling has taken over so much of their lives that they are not sure if they can ever recapture their sense of being without betraying the child they had lost. For some time, this wasmy feeling. I felt that I didn't want to be around and accept anyone into my life that had a child, as I would be betraying Ashley. This feeling doesn't go away overnight. It takes time and patience for one to deal with on their own timeline.

Angry that parents fail at being a responsible parent...

Many people who have lost a child (or even those who haven't) can relate to the feeling that some parents just shouldn't be parents. I have heard everything: that there should be a test, an IQ test, something that would determine if the individuals are suitable to be parents.

Unfortunately, there isn't one.

I can't begin to tell you how many times while growing up that I saw parents that I didn't think were suitable. As I moved into adulthood I watched with disgust as parents left their children at home so they could go out drinking and partying.

Take a trip through any mall or grocery store and I'm sure you will come across people like this, and the feeling that develops can be rather difficult to control. I can't begin to tell you how many times I've wanted to walk up to one of these parents and treat them the same way that they are treating the child that they are supposed to be caring for. We have all seen these types of parents. These are not the ones who are simply trying to instill some sort of control or respect in their child; these are the parents who are acting worse than the children themselves.

Fortunately, I have controlled my anger enough not to place my hands around their necks and choke the life out of them, but I have made it a point to make some rather interesting comments to them regarding their highly skilled parenting qualities. Though I know this wasn't the best course of action, or the most suitable, I can't say that I didn't gleam some sense of satisfaction. Unfortunately, the satisfaction just doesn't last long enough, and the anger continues to fester and build up inside. All you want to do is find some way, some manner, to release the anger that you have.

Ready to explode...

From my personal experience, I know that the angrier I became, the more I wanted to start breaking, throwing and smashing things. This could be because I have always pent up my frustrations until I was ready to explode. But for others, this could just be the overwhelming feeling that all this anger develops.

As this anger develops, often you want some sort of release like I mentioned above. Sometimes your able to do that, while other times you may not have the opportunity to release that anger. Many books attempt to say that this is not a healthy release and that you should take the time and speak about this. Many try to bury this within themselves and end up trying to hide this feeling. When we bury or hide this feeling we take it to our personal Cave.

Later, I will talk about releasing a portion of that anger. I say a portion, because as I have found in myself, and while talking with others, that some of that anger never seems to go away. If you remember earlier in the book, I mentioned the boy with the rubber coin purse. I may not hate him like I once did, but to this day I still have a little bit of anger toward him and his parents.

So, what happens next, you're angry at everything and everyone, you're tired of dealing with and being around people, you're ready to escape…escape to your Cave.

Chapter Five

Into the Cave

Within you there is a stillness and a sanctuary to which you can retreat at any time and be yourself, ~ Hermann Hesse

Into the Cave is the best way I can explain delving into one's self- that inward retreat that so many of us venture into for short periods of time, or, for some in certain situations, extended periods of time. Caves are not normally known for being bright and cheery; they usually tend to be dark, cold and dreary. Think of how many animals escape to a cave, or how many movies see where people are wandering into a cave to either find a treasure or to escape some sort of danger. Just like animals or movie characters, we tend to escape to the cave. We use the cave as an area to retreat and protect ourselves from any harm that is approaching. We tend to treat the cave as a sanctuary of sorts, a wall of protection, a barrier that one establishes to keep others away.

Who enters the cave...

Throughout my entire life I used my internal cave as a sanctuary to escape. I would escape from a difficult situation in an effort to find an answer; I would escape from my wife and others close to me so I would not have to talk about what I was feeling or what was on my mind.

After losing Ashley, and realizing that there was no communication in my marriage, I decided to read a book that spoke about women and men being from different planets in our universe but trying to cohabitate on Earth. Although the book did not assist me with the communication issues I was having at the time, the book did share that men retreat inwards until they are ready to communicate with their partner.

Though this book shared that the man is usually the one who retreats inward, I would say that both men and women may retreat into their respected caves for a number of reasons. Especially if an individual has lost a loved one, we will find that escaping to the cave is something that many people do. The reason most people think of the man as the primary person to go to the cave is that they are often the most reluctant to communicate what they are feeling. As society continues to evolve, we see that gender is no longer the dominant factor of who enters the cave; it is often based upon the experiences a person may have throughout their life.

Why the cave...

People find that in the cave they can stop pretending to be someone else or the person everyone expects them to be. The individuals can be themselves. A person can allow their guard to drop and just escape into a safe and comfortable area that allows their mind to wander and process all of the feelings, experiences, ideas, wants and desires that exist. Some find that they are able to retreat into their cave in any situation, others find that they can only find their refuge if certain considerations exist.

Some find the entrance to their cave while sitting at a bar, others at home in a bath, in bed, or tucked away in a private room.

Whatever the situation, finding the way into the cave is not as significant as finding the way out. Once a person enters the cave, a vast number of experiences and emotions may present themselves allowing them to confront things that they normally would not face. Some may face their fears, others may face what is truly on their mind, and for some they may relive past experiences that bring forth feelings of sadness, resentment, helplessness and anger.

My personal cave...

Like so many others, I began retreating to my own cave at a young age. In fact, as a result of many experiences (physical and emotional abuse, and being socially demeaned) I found refuge in my internal cave throughout much of my adolescent life. After I had left home for the military, I understood that I belonged to Uncle Sam, and therefore would keep my opinions and feelings to myself. As I continued to grow socially, I understood what was acceptable to express, what was important to hide, and how to find refuge in my cave system.

When Ashley was in the ICU, I would sit in the waiting room or walk the halls remaining distant from those around me. During this time, I stayed in my cave. I beat myself up over and over from not spending as much time as I felt I should have, wondering what we could have done differently, and wanting to know why and how this could happen. I kept replaying what the doctor had said and continued to question what could be done.

I started to blame the kids, the babysitter, the military, my wife, God and myself for this situation. I tried to figure out why this had happened what I had done to deserve this, what could I have done that could have prevented it. I played out multiple scenarios but continued to come up with the feelings of anger, resentment, blame, guilt and helplessness. Each time I started thinking those thoughts, I would get angry and want to find someway to help my daughter. l was willing to give anything I had, anything I would have made, I would have given my life if I could just swap places with her.

After losing Ashley, I escaped to my cave and found that reminiscing about her and drowning my sorrows in alcohol only made me delve deeper into the midst of my cave. Though surrounded by people, I wanted to be alone; I wanted to find somewhere that I didn't have to speak or deal with others. I wanted to escape the situation that I was in and die inside.

Unfortunately, as many have experienced, being left alone is not something that usually happens and this becomes the reason why we retreat to our caves. In the cave, we can experience the feelings of helplessness, we can get angry, we can speak our minds without the feeling of being judged, we can experience the feelings that we don't share or recognize with others. When we are asked to share or explore those feelings, we immediately wish to shut down, believing these feelings are private and belong inside the cave.

Your cave...

Each of you have your very own personal cave, each of you have your own entry into that cave, and each of you have circumstances that trigger you to automatically drift off to your cave. The challenge is the thoughts that you have while you are in that moment. The thoughts that often occur while you are in the cave begin to gnaw on you and continue to build greater frustration. You want a solution to your problem but none are in sight.

To make matters worse, you continue to have people step in front of you and tell you how sorry they are or how they wish they could do something to help. Of course these people are just trying to help, but they don't realize that they are feeding the anger, the resentment and the guilt that you feel. What they don't realize is that they are keeping you locked up inside the cave. This vicious cycle continues to occur with no foreseeable end, until we find our way to navigate the cave.

Navigating the cave system...

As a child, I ventured into a cave that was dark and had what seemed to be a maze of tunnels which ultimately led nowhere. When I first entered the cave, I was scared. I could not see in front of me. I stayed next to the walls of rock hoping to use the sides as a guide. There was no map, no guide, no light to show me where I was going or how to get there. I had to navigate the cave system alone.

Eventually I found my way out of the cave and like most boys, I ended up going back but found myself out faster that next time.

Later in life, I started scuba diving. After a couple hundred dives, both my wife, Christy, and I were invited to attend a cave diving class. Now, as of the writing of this book, we haven't taken up that challenge (yet), but we have started reading, researching and purchasing the exuberant amount of additional equipment one needs to navigate through an underwater cave system.

One of the most crucial items that a person needs and must learn how to operate is a line and reel. This line and reel serves as the guideline to help you navigate out of the cave. Sometimes in our lives we need that guideline, but the challenge of asking for it or using it may go against our nature.

Growing up, I never asked for help. Call it pride, call it stubbornness, or maybe I was just being dumb, but asking for help was not even a consideration. My mother raised me with the mindset that you work hard, you don't ask for help, and you will be rewarded for your efforts. Heck, I spent the majority of my life thinking that philosophy was correct until I read a book that told me I was wrong, and it made sense!

Years before Ashley was born, I was determined that I could navigate through my own cave no matter the situation and without asking for any assistance. After she died, I still thought that I could navigate my cave on my own. When the members of the Free and Accepted Masons caught me off guard by providing food and cleaning my home, I still did not ask for help of any sort. In fact, it wasn't until ten years after her death that I finally begin opening up and talking about the frustrations I experienced after Ashley's death.

Previously, I had shared the story of how she passed away; I had even worked with other soldiers who had lost their children, but I had never explored how I was dealing with and was coming to terms with her death. I still had not shared a birthday with my new wife and our children, and I would still go through periods of depression. The bouts could last almost two weeks where I wouldn't even speak with them. In fact, I had volunteered to accept orders for temporary duty away from my family and to even deploy to Afghanistan, taking me away from my new family for the first six years of our marriage.

The individual I began sharing some things with was an Army psychologist named Jeff. Jeff worked with the same unit I was assigned, evaluating the measures of stress that was placed on the students of a course that I was teaching.

While traveling with the course, Jeff and I had time to build a friendship. I began talking through how I was coping with Ashley's death. Jeff never told me how to feel, how I should feel, or if I was wrong. Instead, he just listened. He listened with sincerity and just asked simple questions about how I felt and whether or not I would change the various decisions I had made after her death. Jeff was nonjudgmental, and was there to lend an ear.

Of course, there were a few things that I didn't share with Jeff, though I am sure he had already figured them out. I never shared about the drinking; I never shared the direct contemplation of suicide. But I'm sure he had figured it out, as I consistently took opportunities of unnecessary risk.

Without providing direct advice, Jeff was instrumental in helping me navigate through my personal cave. The conversations with him eventually allowed me to share more with my supportive wife, Christy, and further strengthened our marriage.

There are probably friends, family and loved ones who would like the opportunity to assist you in navigating through your personal cave system. And if you are a supporter who happens to be reading this, I will simply say: Remain supportive and willing.

An individual cannot be forced to cope with the emotions and feelings that they experience until they are ready to work through them. If you try to force a person before they are ready, they will just retreat further into their cave.

Just think, it took me ten years before I truly <u>began</u> exploring my feelings and became willing to work through them. When I went to counseling that one time with Ashley's mother, I was frustrated and angry that I was going to listen to someone tell me what to feel and when I should be feeling certain things. My answer to that was simple: retreat. The lesson one can take away from this is that, when they are ready, each person will find the time to receive help navigating out of the cave.

Entering someone else's cave...

This section is for those friends, family and loved ones who desire to help someone through their grieving process.

The first thing you need to keep in mind is that no matter how good the intentions, no matter how good the relationship you may have, if the individual is not ready and willing to have someone assist them, they will not accept the assistance you are offering. As you read through this section, I want you to visualize the yellow caution tape that exists. You should tread lightly. This said, there are usually two ways you can enter into someone else's cave: being invited or barging in.

Being invited into someone else's cave will depend upon the time frame of that individual. For some, the time may be short, for others it may be longer. Each individual is different, and you will need to wait until they are ready. When I started talking to Jeff, I made a conscious effort to share with him how I felt and how I was coping with Ashley's death. While speaking with him, I began opening up to Christy and sharing some of the feelings that continued to manifest with me. One of the most troublesome areas that she had was my feeling of failure as a father. No matter how much she reminded me that the circumstances around Ashley's death were out of my control, I refused to hear it. In fact, my initial reaction was to retreat into my cave. Instead, she took a different approach.

She began asking how I felt now towards our daughters. Of course, my initial response was that I was a failure with our girls as well. But, her persistence paid off as she slowly convinced me that this was not the case. There are times that I may slowly delve back into my cave and think that I am not where I would like to be as a parent, but how many of us truly are. One thing has helped me is to remain grounded by remembering where I came from.

Many situations about so many topics arise where I immediately think of retreating into my cave. This isn't to escape the situation exactly, but rather to give me time to mull it over in my mind. While I may think this helps, I realize it creates a lack of communication between Christy and myself.

Often, she reminds me to think of the instruction book I was handed for our daughters (as most of you know, there isn't one), then she reminds me to think of the examples I had growing up (hmmm, none to really speak of), and then she reminds me that we are traveling this path together and trying to do the best we can. I hate the idea of putting this in print, but you know what.... she is right.

Many have the same situation; we don't receive a handbook for our kids, and there is no handbook for dealing with friends or your own personal grief cycle or cave system. What we have is a support network. We may not always see it, but various support networks exist, and we just have to be willing to accept them.

The second way to enter someone else's cave is by charging in. Unfortunately, all to often this is the approach that is taken without realizing the damage that is being done. Charging in occurs in one of two ways: The well-intentioned subtle approach or the hard, charging, tackle-the-problem, head on approach. In either case, duck and prepare for retaliation.

Some of you may have already experienced the blowback from these approaches, and hopefully the damage was not so severe that a friendship was ruined or family ties broken. Should this be the case, the road to recovery is long and bumpy.

The subtle approach is often used when a family member or friend continues to insist that they are around to help, they insist that they are there if you want to talk, and they slowly begin forcing the conversation upon the bereaved. At times, they may share how hard they are taking all of this, and that they want to share with you that they feel the same way.

I had someone do this in my life, and I stopped talking to her for two years (understand, that was a short period of time, for many it could be a lifetime). That individual happened to be my mother; she wanted me to know that she was feeling the same way for losing her granddaughter and wanted to move through the grief stage together. What she didn't realize is that she was slowly encroaching upon my cave. Like any barricaded wild animal, I did what seemed to come natural: I lashed back.

I immediately moved from the cave to anger and shut down any and all communication between the two of us. Some of you may have already experienced this event; others may be on the borderline right now. In either case, now would be a good time to retreat and allow your friend or loved one the space that they need.

The not-so-subtle approach reminds me of a football player attaching the defensive line, or maybe one of those police officers from the movies who dons a bulletproof vest and charges into a room of villains to be met with a barrage of bullets. I have seen this occur as a friend or a family member feels the grieving individual needs to be dealt a hand of "tough love" in order to move past this whole ordeal. I have heard someone tell a bereaved parent that his or her child was lost. This is God's plan; accept it and move on.

Upon hearing this, I had to hold back from walking up to the individual and knocking them flat on their butt. I couldn't believe that someone not only had the audacity to do this, but to think that this could possibly help. I don't believe that the bereaved parent has ever spoken to this family member since.

So what now...

As either the bereaved, a family member or a loved one the question is always what is next? What do we expect now? What do we do now? Understanding that people want to help, or that they are available to help is a step down the road to recovery.

The question then becomes how long is this going to take, and what can we expect while time is being taken? What I have experienced is that various feelings like resentment, blame and anger continue to fester in the hearts and minds, which returns us to the anger stage, or the stage when we begin to question, Why?

Chapter Six

Why?

One of the most frustrating questions that I had a hard time finding an answer to is, "Why did this happen?" From talking to others, I know that the same question resonates throughout their entire experience with no answer bringing comfort or clarity to the situation.

In my personal experience, I began asking why while my daughter was in the emergency room. I wanted to know why this happened. Why did it have to happen? Why was their change in the crib? Why hadn't the crib been searched? Why did she put the dime in her mouth? Why this and why that, over and over again.

Each time I would think about a why, I would begin to get angry. Each time someone would come up to say they were sorry to me or if they could do anything for me, I would start through the entire process of why over and over again. The "whys" continued to build and my frustration continued to increase. As I started working through the whys, I would eventually transitions from why to angry, to helpless, to angry, to feeling all alone, and back to questioning why again. When I eventually shared the question with those who were close to me or around me at the time, no sufficient answer existed that I was ready to accept. In fact, I'm not sure if I have ever really accepted any answer to the why that is sufficient to me.

Questioning why this occurred….

Probably one of the most often asked question is, "Why did this occur?" I know I was looking for some sort of reason. The fact that my daughter was so young and couldn't truly understand or make choices for herself did not help the situation. It wasn't as if I could have told her not to put things in her mouth and she would have understood. She was still a baby, and knowing what the right and wrong thing to do was just inconceivable.

I could have questioned our friend, the babysitter, about the whole ordeal and why she didn't recheck the crib that she kept in a separate room with the door closed so that no one would go in. I could have gone through a long list of questions that wouldn't have made me feel any better, and would have made her feel even worse. But what would this have accomplished? Heck, it wouldn't have even made me feel good.

We all want to know why this occurred, for those who have lost a loved one in a car accident, there are questions about everything from the road conditions, and their driving ability, distractions, and the list goes on. If only they were more careful, if only they had driven slower, if I had driven them. The 'if this' and 'if that' end up drowning our thoughts as we develop solutions and alternate scenarios that could have been done that would have prevented the loss of our loved one.

Unfortunately, we play these scenarios over and over, wishing that we could have changed the past, thinking that maybe there was something we could have done different, if only we were given the opportunity again. And then we start thinking, "if we could only trade places". What we would give to trade places and be the one dying so that our loved one may go on. We say this unselfishly, not because we are martyrs, but because we believe in giving that opportunity to our child, to our love one. We are the ones who were supposed to make sure that they had a long life and saw us in our old ages; we are the ones who were supposed to protect them so they could have a long and happy life and experience new things that we had dreamed for them. When we start having these feelings, we begin to wonder why this had to happen to me.

Questioning why did this occur to me....

Days from turning 25 years old, I was ready to trade places with my daughter. I wasn't frustrated, I was angry that this had happened and continued to rack my brain trying to find some rhyme or reason for it. Many of us have been there, many of us feel that we need to put the blame on ourselves or punish ourselves by trying to understand why this occurred. I have read books and heard people tell me that I should not blame myself or question why this occurred to me.

Well, the truth of the matter is that is ridiculous! Just because someone feels good about themself, telling you that you shouldn't harness any of the blame or that you shouldn't wonder why this occurred to you, doesn't mean that these thoughts aren't going through your head. And, if you weren't thinking them before, those thoughts are in your head now.

The problem I came to realize eventually is that when I started dwelling on why this occurred to me, I began focusing the attention on myself rather than on Ashley. When this happened, I began feeling selfish. I was thinking how could this happen to me, when I should have been thinking how could this have happened to her.

I'm not saying that we shouldn't think about why this happened to us; I am saying that we need to try to keep our perspective and remember what is important and why.

It's only natural that we experience the thoughts of why this occurred to us. We will all wonder, we will all question and we will all get upset when we can't find a sufficient answer. Some people may be different, but when I couldn't find the answer I was looking for I began questioning God.

Questioning God....

This section may be controversial to some, depending upon your religious beliefs. What I am sharing is my experience, my thoughts, and even some of the similar experiences that others have gone through. I feel that writing this is extremely important, as many of us who have lost a child have heard someone at one time or another say this was God's will or part of His plan. This is definitely not the easiest thing to hear after losing a loved one.

Growing up, I was taught that we don't question God, that He has a time and a purpose for everything. When Ashley was lying in the emergency room, I began questioning God. When Ashley was lying in the infant intensive care unit, I questioned God. When I gave permission for the doctor to take my baby off life support, I questioned God. I questioned why this had to happen to such an innocent girl, I questioned why He couldn't just take me instead, I questioned what I had done that was so terrible that I had to be punished. That was finally my resolution, God was so angry with me that I had to be punished and He took my daughter as my punishment.

The mind is an incredible machine that we can program based upon the data that we provide. I wanted to blame someone or something so badly that I developed reasons that I was the one to blame for my daughters' death. Because I couldn't find any rationale, I created rationale, using God and any and all events that occurred in my past to develop a plausible blame line that I could accept as to why my daughter died. Though I questioned why God had taken my daughter, I was relieved when I developed an answer that held me responsible.

After speaking to other fathers, I found that many of them had also questioned God during and after the tragedy. Each individual wanted an answer from God as to why this occurred. When the only answer received was that this was part of His plan, they, like me, were able to rationalize some past event to use as the reason that they lost their child. The challenge resulting from this rationale is twofold. First, we begin thinking this is about us (back to the selfishness), and second, we create another and more serious problem that we or our surviving loved ones, friends and families may have to deal with. The rationale that we are to blame creates a self-destructive nature within us that becomes volatile and dangerous for our loved ones and ourselves. When I found comfort in blaming myself, I found myself on a self-destructive path that included drinking and thoughts of suicide as I attempted to determine if life itself was worth continuing on.

Questioning why to continue on, what is the worth...

With the true love of my life gone, I began wondering if life itself was worth living. I wasn't speaking with my wife, as she was trying to share with me what she received out of grief counseling and how I should be feeling and acting. Work didn't seem to matter and I could perform my job with little thought and even presence if I so desired. My friends were distant; they didn't know what they could do to help me or if they could help me at all. Their normal reply was they were sorry, and we all know how those words would just get me worked up and angry. The questioning would continue, but this time questioning if life was worth continuing.

I had contemplated suicide. As part of the feeling of helplessness and loneliness, the questioning of why should I go on came forward, and I found myself contemplating the idea of shooting myself in my daughter's bedroom.

Was this going to solve anything? I guess the idea that I would not have to suffer through this ordeal anymore was somewhat comforting, but I realized that what my family was going through with the loss of my daughter would only be magnified if I were to take my life as well. I began thinking of all the people that I knew, and even those I didn't, who came out to support me as I was going through this horrible experience. I thought of those that could never imagine experiencing something like this, and though they didn't understand, their intentions were for the best and honorable. Honor. Hmmm. What honor would I bring upon myself as a soldier if I decided to take the cowardly way out of a situation by committing suicide. What honor would be in that?

I began getting angry again. Angry that I contemplated suicide, and angry that I had no answers as to what I should do next. I was confused and wanted someone to give me the next step to take to move through this trying time. Although I may have wanted this, I wasn't ready to have anyone help me with this problem. I knew that something needed to be done, but would become angry that I didn't know what it was. I wanted someone to tell me the next step, but how could they if I wouldn't let them in or get close to me.

Years later, and after speaking with other fathers, I realized that this was a normal sequence of events. We all knew that we wanted some reason to go on, but knew there was nothing that anyone could say that we wanted to hear as a reason. Though we wanted someone to say something to us, I believe it is our own self-discovery as to why we need to go on that motivates and allows us to move into the future. But, until then, we just become angry that we want a reason but just don't have it.

Chapter Seven

Angry again

The stages one goes through during the grieving process has no time line. As events happen and our senses bring forth various memories, we may find ourselves going through the cycle in a matter of minutes, days, weeks or even longer. There is not rhyme or reason; no cookie cutter answer to how long each individual will remain in a certain stage. Through talking with others and my own first-hand experience, I found that I returned to the anger stage on several occasions (alright, maybe a little more). Often, this return was after I experienced the previous two stages of the Cave and Questioning. Those two stages would have me so riled up that I returned to the anger stage before going through the entire grieving cycle again.

Alright to be angry...

I mentioned that it is alright to be angry; it is natural and something that everyone goes through. Unfortunately, I have heard people say and have read books that tell people that they shouldn't be angry and not to act upon those feelings. For those who have read this or heard this I have a special exercise for you to conduct, just in case you have listened to that advice in the past. Here is a step-by-step exercise that I would like you to do right now.

1. Fold back the corner of this page in the book.
2. Stand up.
3. Lift the book to about shoulder level.
4. Throw the book to the ground.

This may sound silly to some, others may be to embarrassed to do it, and for some of you- you may have to go find the book after throwing it across the room. It is all right to be angry; you should be after losing a child. How dare someone tell you that you don't have the right to get angry or find some way to release the anger. I was so angry that I drank, contemplated shooting myself, put my fists through some walls, and finally took up Judo so I could throw people and choke them out. All of this just to find some way to release the anger that I had balled up inside of me.

When I first stepped into the Judo dojo in Fayetteville, North Carolina, I knew that I wanted some way to release all of the pent-up anger. This wasn't my first time walking into a martial arts studio. In fact, I had trained quite a bit from my teenage years to my current time in the military. What I did know was that Judo, which is translated into English as the "Gentle Way", was not as gentle as one would think.

Just think of having someone about the same size of you lifting you off the ground and throwing you over their shoulder so while you come crashing to the ground. Again, not the most gentle of activities in which to participate, but for someone who was so frustrated with everyone around him that I had considered taking my own life, I thought that maybe this would be the right answer for me.

Looking back now, I don't know if I started Judo as a method to release my anger or if it was my way of punishing myself. But, after the first week of being thrown all over the dojo, I was hobbling around with bruises all over my body. So, if the goal was to punish myself, I'm sure I had accomplished that. And as a measure to release my anger, I was fortunate to have a wonderful instructor and training partners who would allow me to attempt to bite off more than I could chew, which usually resulted with me flying through the air once again. For me, this is what I needed. I needed some constructive way to release the anger I had bottled up inside me.

Everyone needs some manner of release or they become a stick of unstable dynamite, ready to explode. The challenge is finding a way to release your anger without hurting yourself or someone else. I know people who have never been runners, but found running or exercising became their way to release the anger. I know others who explored martial arts, boxing or mixed martial arts as an avenue to release their anger. I have met some who have beaten up pillows in private, leaving them unrecognizable. Others I have met took on some less physical approaches such as writing, journaling, painting, woodcarving or carpentry. No matter the venue or the type of activity, I think it is important for each person to find their own way to release their anger with some sort of control.

Control is extremely important. Anger can be a fickle feeling, especially when we are attempting to release some of it. When I speak about control, I want you to consider how you are going to release your anger and who is going to be around when you do this.

The problem when we release our anger in an uncontrolled manner is the risk of hurting someone else. Initially, this isn't something we take into consideration, but once it is done we will end up regretting how we acted against another person.

While practicing Judo, I learned about control and how the simplest move can change the momentum of a situation. I learned that if I lack control even the most inexperienced player could easily defeat me. When I stepped out onto the mat and played with a level of control, I was able to defend myself, and depending on the circumstances, even win at times. What I learned was that both control on the mat and control in my life were essential to not feel like I was being thrown down all of the time. Learning this lesson took a lot of time, which didn't seem to help my immediate situation. And as a result, I wanted to share with you some of the mistakes and lessons that I learned while being angry.

During the anger phase, one may find that a lack of communication occurs and resentment grows at an extremely rapid pace. My wife and I stopped speaking after Ashley died and while we were each working through our grief processes.

She wanted to talk about what was going on and what she had learned from the councilor and how we could manage our way through our bereavement. I, on the other hand, wanted to retreat to my cave and not have any discussions as I felt as if I had failed in my role as a husband and father. As we spoke less, the distance grew between us, eventually resulting in divorce. The lesson I learned through that experience is that communication, no matter how little, is extremely important.

Later in life, as I spoke with other families who had lost children, I conveyed how the lack of communication can drive a wedge in the marriage. I shared that though communication was not wanted or needed at the time, simple little things like a note to remind each other that they love each other, or a small act like holding a hand can be enough. You see the subtle acts; the little things mean so much during this time that just a short note saying you love the other person could be enough to keep a marriage together.

In my current marriage, I have taken this lesson to heart. When we may be experiencing a trying time, or when the anniversary of Ashley's death nears, my wife and I know that a simple act speaks volumes to each of us.

Communication is vital in a relationship, but many become some complacent that they forget to enjoy each other's company and just talk. This isn't something that is easy to do, especially if you have just suffered a loss, but this is something that you may want to keep in the back of your mind.

The other area that creates a significant problem between the bereaved and their loved ones is the feeling of resentment. Previously, I mentioned how I resented being around other people with children, I resented being in the same store or location as parents who I deemed were unfit or just not worthy of being a parent, this was only the beginning. Not only did I not want to be around children or people with children, but I would have absolutely terrible thoughts about them.

I can tell you that I wasn't proud of the thoughts at all, but they were natural to how I was feeling at the time. After speaking to others who have lost children, I was amazed how they all felt similar to the way I did. They could relate. What I learned from this experience was that although people won't share or speak of the horrible things they are thinking or even wishing onto others, the thoughts are somewhat natural to experience. Of course, because no one vocalizes these specific feelings, we end up thinking that something is wrong with us.

The blame game...

During this stage of anger, not only did the resentment resurface, but I also started to blame other people for the situation I was experiencing. Because Ashley was still just a baby, I found that the blame I cast was toward my wife, the babysitter, the doctors, anyone that I could find that would allow me to channel my anger towards someone else. Though I know it takes two to have a baby, I began blaming her for wanting to try to have another child after we had already lost one. I know that this wasn't rational and I know that I wanted our daughter just as bad as she did, but rationale was not present and I wanted someone else to blame beside myself. I blamed her for having a job that forced her to drop our daughter off at a babysitter. Again, not rational as part of the reason for her needing to have a job was that we moved to North Carolina because of an opportunity I had with the military.

This ended up increasing my frustration with joining the military. Because if I hadn't joined the military, I wouldn't have met my wife, which meant I wouldn't have gotten married, which meant I wouldn't have had Ashley, which ultimately meant my daughter would not have died. As stated earlier, none of this was rational, but it gave me reason to focus on being angry at something or someone else for a short period of time.

During one episode of anger, I laid some blame on the babysitter. I blamed her for watching two other children besides Ashley and her own. I blamed her that the other children were allowed to open the door to the room Ashley's playpen was kept. And as I started laying blame, I realized I wasn't as upset with her as I was the two other boys she babysat and their parents. These two children, in the best of terms, were your classic undisciplined brats. The two boys would not listen to the babysitter, and felt they could do as they pleased. The babysitter would tell them not to go into the spare room that Ashley's playpen was kept, but, in typical fashion, they would open the door to show their rebellion. The evening before these boys opened the door to enter the room, the babysitter had told them to get out, and the boys threw a temper tantrum by throwing their rubber coin purse across the room spreading coins everywhere, leaving the babysitter to move them out of the room and go clean up the coins.

Of course, while she was picking up the coins, the boys moved to the kitchen to see what other damage they could immerse themselves in.

So, as I thought of this, I blamed the two boys and their parents who didn't understand how to rear or discipline children. I was so angry with the boys and their parents that if they had been standing in front of me when I was at the hospital or right after Ashley had died, I probably would have killed them.

Now, I'm not just expressing words about this, when you truly blame another person for being responsible for the death of a loved one, the rationale is gone and I wanted to kill the parents and the boys themselves. Part of my healing process was to get passed these thoughts, but as I reflect on that incident as I write this now, I still get upset.

The babysitter...

As I have shared my story with others, one question is often asked when speaking about blame and becoming angry. I am often asked why I don't blame the babysitter.

Earlier I mentioned passing thoughts of blame, but nothing really aimed at her or her family. The babysitter, her husband, and two boys were stationed in Hawaii with my wife and I at the same time. Her husband worked in the same unit and in the same platoon as I did. He and I had shared many unique military experiences together, and our two families had shared many activities. When we moved to North Carolina, they arrived shortly after. We continued participating in numerous events together, from Trick-or-Treating to fall hayrides. Because she was staying home with her sons until they were old enough to go to school, she was more than willing to babysit Ashley.

Although we did pay her a small stipend to babysit Ashley, this was probably nowhere near the amount that would have covered the expense her and her family spent on my daughter. There would be times that I would pick Ashley up after work and she would have not one, but multiple new outfits if they had to run out to the store and saw something they thought she would look cute in. Their sons always wanted to have their parents purchase new toys for Ashley so they could see a new expression or just hear her laugh and see her smile.

On that tragic day, she stood up and rushed to hug me as I walked into the ER waiting room, before my wife had a chance. While waiting, she cried with us and spent almost every waking moment at the hospital until a decision had to be made. Unfortunately, once the decision was made, neither her nor her husband could feel comfortable being around my wife or me.

I attempted to call on different occasions, but received no response from either. That time was difficult for both my family and theirs, and I am sure that she felt she needed to blame herself and may have felt that internally we blamed her for Ashley's death.

On the contrary, I think that they may have assisted my grieving process, and hopefully would have assisted in theirs and solidified the fact that I putno blame on anyone in their family.

As I write this, I have considered attempting to get in touch with her again, especially since her husband has passed away in combat. I have considered sending a letter, attempting to connect on social media, but feel none of this would be as appropriate as visiting her in person. Maybe one day I will visit her, and should she still hold any pent up grief or guilt about Ashley, help her work through these issues. I wish we had remained in touch those many years ago. I would have liked to have been there as support for her when she lost her husband.

This situation is unfortunate, as I believe the loss of communication was a result of their family feeling we blamed them for Ashley's death. This is where blame can cause so many problems that we may not think of while we are grieving. The problem with blaming others is that we end up holding them responsible at times, even when they may not have had anything to do with the situation or they were involved inadvertently.

I have spoken with families that have lost their child as a result of SIDS, shaken baby syndrome, car accidents, drug overdose, murder and freakish accidents. No matter the situation, we all end up wanting to harness a portion of the blame ourselves and find a way to channel a portion of blame onto another person, no matter how detrimental this could be.

A few years after losing Ashley, I was asked to speak to a father who was a member of a Special Forces Group residing in North Carolina.

Special Forces dad...

Members of the United States Army Special Forces go through rigorous selection and training that test both their mental and physical stamina. These individuals go through grueling tests of strength and endurance to ensure that they have the intestinal fortitude to survive and endure in hostile environments. Many individuals have seen movies or documentaries about these men, but until you spend time with them and truly get to know them you don't really understand the specific nuances that each of these men have.

I met one of these unique individuals a few years after Ashley died. I was asked to speak to him by fellow military members who knew that I lost a daughter. This father, (I'll call Jamie), had lost his teenage son to a drug overdose.

Jamie and I had met previously and he had heard through the grapevine that I had lost a child, but, as with most people, this subject was considered too taboo to speak of. When Jamie was reluctant to speak with anyone after he had lost his son, especially the members of his close-knit team, it wasn't too far-fetched for a mutual friend to ask if I would speak with Jamie.

Jamie was both embarrassed and bitter that he had lost his son from a drug overdose. He was angry at his son for using drugs; he was angry at himself for not realizing it; he was angry with himself and the military for traveling and being away all of the time; he was angry at the drug dealers who had sold to his son.

Jamie and I always met out in public, either at a restaurant, a bar or coffee shop. I accepted this; I knew that going into the home could be a challenging situation for anyone who recently lost a child. While speaking with Jamie, the anger was extremely evident and the fact that I wasn't trying to tell him not to be angry ended up allowing him to vent and open up to me.

As he vented his anger, he shared how upset he was at his son and how guilty he felt for being upset with him. He was furious that he hadn't seen the signs or, more specifically, that he hadn't been around to spend more time with his son and identify the signs of drug use. The guilt was evident, but the most disturbing fact was that he believed something needed to be done about the drug dealers and the local drug problem in the city.

As I commiserated with him, I could see that there was something more that was left unsaid. As I pressed that police needed to take a more active role, he stated that if the police didn't, someone else should. When I questioned if that someone should be him, I recognized the same expression of hopelessness that I had when I had considered committing suicide.

I asked him a simple question: "what was the plan?" And there it was, Jamie had shared that over the past three months he had been collecting "intelligence" where he was going to raid the home of the drug dealers who had sold his son the drugs. At home, Jamie had detailed plans of the home, the number of people inside, and what equipment he would need to conduct his own personal suicide mission and kill the individuals he blamed for his son's death.

As we spoke, we discussed his wife and his other son and how they would respond to not only losing one family member, but losing a husband and a father as well. His answer was that this is something that they had already planned for with him being in the military. This was hard to argue with as I have discussed the same with my wife, Christy, and it is something most military members prepare their families for.

We discussed the difference of dying in combat and dying on this noble mission of revenge. We discussed other options, but none were as appealing to him as to make those that took his son suffer. With the focus remaining on his wife and other son, Jamie eventually decided that instead of killing the dealers, he would turn over the information he collected to the sheriff's department.

Now whether or not he turned the videos and photos over, I don't know. What I do know is that I ended up seeing Jamie a few years later in a Forward Operating Base in Afghanistan doing what he did best, collecting information and planning out an attack against insurgents threatening the lives of Americans and Afghans alike.

Everyone can find someone to blame or hold responsible, the question is what action they will take when they identify a person to blame for the loss of their loved one. Jamie could have lost more than a son if he had gone through with his plan for revenge.

I have met others who have gone in debt going to court in order to find some satisfaction that another person is guilty or considered to blame for the death of a loved one. Ultimately, my anger and my blaming of others cost me a marriage, and years of silence with other family members.

I don't have regrets. Each experience has taught me something new and has allowed me to grow and help others. But, as I have learned speaking with others, their blame has cost them far more. Asking the question of how much you are willing to risk is not a valid question, because when I lost my daughter I was willing to risk everything. The question I would pose: "Is placing blame more important than learning to deal with the death you are grieving?"

Why are we angry again...

As I reread the question above discussing the importance of placing blame, I have mixed feelings. Yes, initially I want to hold someone else accountable. And yes, I want to manage my way through this grief process. In fact, I want both and am starting to become upset if I can't have both, or maybe because one is more important than the other. Either way, just the thought of deciding is enough to have me or anyone else become upset and angry again.

The feeling that we have to choose to move on is enough for any rational person to become angry, never mind a person who is grief-stricken and disturbed by the loss of a child or loved one. When I heard someone tell me that I needed to move on, I became angry and felt they had no right to tell me what my personal timeline should be.

I think this is one of the hardest areas to work through. I felt I was betraying or forgetting my daughter and didn't want to do that at all. Years had to go by before I could move past the idea of betraying my feelings for her, and even now, as I write this, I wonder 'What if', and occasionally question if I have dismissed her or if she is still with me today. These are passing thoughts, as I always return to the same answer.

I miss my daughter and still wish she were with me today.

Chapter Eight

Acceptance

Initially, I named this chapter *Coming to Terms*, but as I thought about it more, I realized that the title *Acceptance* was better suited; it is what I was truly finding. For me, after going through the cycle (sometimes quickly and sometimes rather slowly) I finally had to come to terms with accepting that my baby girl was not coming back to me.

For any logical person understanding that a loved one who dies isn't coming back makes total sense, but for me, someone who was grieving and didn't want to accept that my baby girl was gone, it was not the easiest thing to digest. I couldn't bring myself to accept the fact that she was dead and gone, I was hoping that the longer I could resist this fact, the less chance I had of truly accepting she was gone.

I just can't believe it...

While pacing the floor of the hospital intensive care unit, I knew that Ashley had a slim chance of breathing on her own. I knew that the inevitable would be said to me, and I knew that she would be gone from me forever. And although I knew this, I just couldn't believe that she was gone, I couldn't believe that I wouldn't have her back home crawling around the house and trying to stand up on her own. I didn't want to accept that she would be gone and I wouldn't have her again.

I am the one who was supposed to die before her; I was her father, and I was a day away from turning 25 and couldn't believe that her life has ended before mine. Hell, I was a soldier who spent his time in the infantry, rappelling from helicopters and jumping from airplanes. I was the one who was supposed to go before her; she was supposed to be my legacy.

Talking with various fathers who have lost their children, all have related that the idea of accepting the death of their child was one of the more challenging and frustrating times during their grief process. In my personal experience, I started going through my own grief cycle all over again, and with those that I have talked to, many related how they were angry after having to accept this fact.

Many parents shared how they would sit there thinking that this just couldn't have happened, and that this was a horrible nightmare they were experiencing, and just couldn't believe this was happening to them. While talking to many bereaved fathers and mothers, they all have shown subtle signs of anger, frustration or remorse when they share what they were feeling when they finally accepted the loss of their child.

When we talked about when they accepted the fact that their child was gone forever, I could see this expression change as they remember that exact moment when they had to accept the death. The expression relates to a specific feeling, and though I am able to empathize, this is not enough. There is so much more included into this memory and emotion.

The feeling is hard to explain, the emptiness is something that I just can't seem to fit into words, but anyone who has lost an extremely close loved one understands the emptiness. Compound that emptiness with the hopes, desires and dreams of a lifetime that you had hoped to spend with that person and you only just begin to scratch the surface as to what this experience feels like.

What could have been...

I think one of the hardest challenges for me was the constant thought of what could have been. Each and every one of us has hopes and desires for our children. I haven't met a person yet who said that they never had a passing thought of what their child could become. Many parents have specific hopes and goals that their child will become involved with certain sports or activities that they were involved in as a child, or wish they had the opportunity to become involved.

How often do we see proud parents go out and purchase merchandise of a certain sports team or their Alma Mater? This isn't because they think the color looks good on the baby, this is because they have hopes that the child will either go to that specific university, enjoy following that specific team, or become an enthusiast of whatever the merchandise represents.

As I reflect back now on what aspirations I had for Ashley, I can't think of anything specific. What I do recall is that I wanted her to have a better life than I had growing up; I wanted her to take every opportunity provided so she could be successful. I know I had hoped that she would have multiple interests, and become involved in many activities that would keep her and me, as a parent, busy. I wanted her to be smart, athletic, and beautiful and have common sense. I hoped that she would achieve her dreams and I wanted to be there to see that happen. I had hoped of one day accepting the fact that I would have to walk her down the aisle and give her away to a man that I had already threatened multiple times to be good and take care of her. All of these things I looked forward to, but now would not have that opportunity.

Sports dad...

During various conversations with parents, I met a father (I'll call Mike) who had the typical dreams of seeing his son participate in little league, pee wee football, and become actively involved in sports throughout his formidable years. Mike had purchased his son jerseys of his favorite college and professional teams, the baby room was filled with sports paraphernalia, and the toys were all geared towards sports and hand eye coordination. Mike was proud of the baby room and would show this off to all of his friends and family. Mike recorded multiple videos of his son playing with balls and other toys that would one day lead this boy to a great sports career. At the age of four, while retrieving a ball that rolled into the street, Mike's son was truck by a passing car.

Mike, like any parent, went through a flurry of emotions. When I spoke to him about his aspirations for his son, he was disappointed that he would never see his son at a high school baseball or football game. Even worse, Mike continued to blame himself for his son's death. If he didn't buy the toys, if he didn't encourage and praise his son while playing ball, if he just didn't want to see his son play sports like he did, maybe his son would be there today. If his own feeling of guilt was not enough, Mike lost his wife as she blamed him for giving their son the toys and encouraging his interest. Mike blamed himself for his son's death and all because of what could have been.

Motorcycle couple...

Being in the military I have been around my share of individuals who love motorcycles. I have come to realize that there are those who like motorcycles (motorcycle enthusiast) and those that *live* motorcycles. In my experiences, I had the opportunity to meet a motorcycle couple that had great aspirations for their daughter to love motorcycles as much as they did. This couple prepared the entire baby room in a motorcycle motif. This room didn't just have pictures, and motorcycle memorabilia, these parents went all out and purchased motorcycle linens to compliment the handmade motorcycle crib they had built.

They were excited and were looking forward to a lifetime of travel and fun experiences as their daughter became older. Unfortunately for this couple, their baby died one evening of Sudden Infant Death Syndrome (SIDS), taking away their hopes and dreams of sharing their passion with their child.

So many parents throughout the world have so many hopes, dreams and desires for their children to fulfill that when they experience a tragic loss they are frequently reminded of what could have been. For the father, he stopped attending and watching any sports related activities, as this was just a haunting reminder of the loss of his son. Many parents end up giving up elements of their lives as a form of punishing themselves for losing their child.

Today, January 14, 2012 (13 years the anniversary of my daughters death) I dismissed a morning and afternoon of previously made plans. Was this my way of punishing myself? Maybe a feeling of guilt that I was going to do something for me on the day my daughter died? This is still something I am learning to bear as I continue to progress though my healing and grief process.

It should have been me...

Earlier in this book, I related how I thought that it should have been me to die rather than my daughter. I was turning 25 and had enough different experiences that could have lasted others a lifetime. I had traveled places, seen things, and done things that others may have only dreamed about experiencing. When Ashley was in the emergency room I prayed. I wished, and desired that I could trade places with my little girl just to give her a chance at life, a chance to have just some of the experiences I had. I know there was nothing I could have done. I know there was no way that I could have traded places, but I wished I had that opportunity to trade places with my daughter.

I have spoken with single parents and couples alike that also would have traded anything to exchange places with their child. I think some of the hardest conversations were with parents who were in accidents with their child and they lived although the child did not. They have related repeatedly that they would willingly have traded places with their loved one, since they are overridden with the guilt of being a survivor. Unfortunately, in many of these circumstances, the parents aren't the only ones to bear the weight of this burden. Often, if there were other children present, involved or not with the accident, this begins to overshadow them as they continue on in life. What I later came to realize was that this wasn't only subject to the siblings who may have been alive at the same time, but may also end up reflecting on children whom come about later in life.

It should have been me...part II...

I can best relate with the guilt and wishing to trade places from a parent's perspective. However, when speaking with siblings who lost a brother or sister, I learned they wished they could have traded places for a number of reasons. Just as with some parents, these siblings are overshadowed by guilt that they lived and their sibling died. I have met with some who had survived an accident while the other sibling did not. I have met those who felt guilty for not having the strength, knowledge, presence, maturity, you name it to save their sibling from whatever cause of death was experienced.

One of the worse things I have discovered in talking to various siblings is when they, especially younger siblings, feel they are living in the shadow of their deceased older brother or sister. When a a parent idolizes the deceased sibling, or tells the other child that they are not good enough or can't live up to what the other sibling accomplished, perpetuates this feeling. As a result, the surviving sibling begins to wish they were the one who died and wish they could exchange places so they no longer live in the shadow of another. There comes a time, as a child becomes older and endures greater frustration, the child will either distance themselves from the parent, seek attention from an undesirable manner, or even take their own lives. From talking with both these children and the parents, I understand that the comparison was not intentional, but the feelings created were the same.

Am I not good enough, do you love them more...

Previously, I spoke about how a sibling may feel they are living in the shadow of another child that was part of the family previously. In my situation, my children inherited a parent who had previously lost a child. A few years after losing Ashley, I ended up divorcing and then remarried. My wife, Christy, had two daughters who were six and four years of age when we met. Choosing to marry was a hard choice, especially with children involved and one that was only a year and a half older than Ashley. When we married, Christy slowly shared with the girls that I had a daughter who passed away.

The oldest, ever so tactful, approached and asked if I missed her. After answering yes, the youngest approached and asked if I still loved my daughter. After answering yes, she asked if I loved her. I shared that I didn't just love her mommy, but loved her and her sister, which brought a smile to her small face. With that, they both ran off to play. Christy apologized for the questions, but felt they should know. Although I understood, the questions developed a feeling of guilt that I had to tend with yet once again.

In the beginning of our marriage, we celebrated each girl's birthday and Christy's as well. After two years, the girls were confused as to why I didn't have a birthday. Could it be that their Papa just never aged? When finally asked one day, they learned I didn't celebrate my birthday because I associated it with Ashley's death. Although they complained to their mother how this was unfair, because they wanted to celebrate and show me that they loved me, I remained unwavering about not celebrating my birthday.

For nine years, Christy and our two daughters respected my wishes to not celebrate my birthday. Always careful as to what to say, and never wanting to appear selfish, my new daughters were understanding and attempted to be supportive as much as they could. Yet, in hushed conversation with their mother, they voiced concerns that I loved Ashley more than I loved them.

When I heard these words, I was conflicted. I did not want my daughters to feel as if they were not important, but at the same time I felt guilty for betraying the memory of my daughter by replacing her with my new daughters. I had the answer all along, but accepting the answer was not something I wanted to do. I did not want to accept that Ashley was gone, and that my two new daughters were replacing her. Then I realized I didn't have to accept that.

What I needed to accept is that I didn't have one daughter that died, and two new ones who were with me. What I needed to accept was that I had three daughters. Though one was no longer with me, I still had two daughters that I could cherish care for. After finally coming to this realization, long talks with both Christy and Jeff, and continuing to work on this book, I finally opened up and allowed them to give me cards and say Happy Birthday after almost ten years of marriage.

This year, going on eleven years of marriage we progressed to muffins in the morning, a present (where I can sit and work on the books I am writing), cards, and a nice family dinner. Both of my daughters understand the importance of the day prior to my birthday and are extremely supportive. They equally understand that sharing my birthday is a reciprocal display of love.

What I just shared took years to reach, and during those years there were many setbacks that developed unintentionally. Each event in their lives, the first day of school, graduating from kindergarten, birthday parties, and so on were rather trying times for me. I remember when Christy and I decided we were going to teach our oldest how to ride a bicycle. This was fine for a while, but I had to step away at one point because I began to cry. I was upset that I would never have the opportunity to teach Ashley how to ride a bicycle. I think it was at that moment that I realized I needed to cherish the time I had with my two daughters do every activity I could with them. This was not easy, and truly accepting that I had my other two daughters to do things with is often easier said then done. Fortunately for me, both girls understand that I love them immensely and accept them as my daughters, and when the week of Ashley's death and my birthday comes around they know that in a way they lost a sister as well.

And yet another grief process to deal with...

As a parent, this brings a whole other challenge, trying to balance your personal grieving process while understanding that children are grieving as well. Just like spouses may not grieve alike, children could grieve in an entirely different manner altogether. I have spoken with adults who lost siblings when they were younger; these individuals they were often confused to how they should act after their sibling passed away.

I have found that each situation depends on certain aspects of their home lives. As the variables changed for each individual, so did the grieving process. Some were able to see both parents grieve, while others did not. Some came from a home with a single parent, whereas others had both parents. Some were involved with church, extracurricular activities, sports, etc. that all had to deal with or involve time, and other relationships that influenced the grieving process.

Each child dealt with something different as they experienced a loss, and each found different experiences to embrace that assisted them through the process. As parents, we must remember that they are experiencing the same feelings we are, they just may have a more challenging time expressing these feelings.

Chapter Nine

Finding Closure

When writing this chapter I had mixed ideas for the title and finally settled on *Finding Closure*. Closure is what most people expect to occur when one grieves. An individual comes to terms that their loved one has passed away, and when the elusive closure is achieved, everything is miraculously supposed to go back to normal.

Although this seems cut and dry, not even the Hollywood film industry is able to portray that simple synopsis in their movies. Instead, finding closure is just that: a search, a quest, a discovery, or any other synonym that portrays a lengthy and ongoing process.

My personal journey towards closure...

After losing Ashley, I could not imagine accepting her death, coming to terms with her being gone, or finding closure. In fact, I attempted to travel down a destructive path as a means to end my own life in an effort to avoid finding closure and moving forward. When I first met Christy, I found a woman with whom I could communicate with on at least two different levels.

The first was through our normal conversations, and the second was through the use of sign language. Any conversations we had that seemed difficult to verbalize, we would immediately transition into the expressive sign language. This ended up becoming an outlet for me to express and share how I was feeling and what was on my mind without ever having to actually say the words. Sign language became my emotional language.

After seeing each other for a while and much debate, Christy decided things were serious enough to introduce me to her daughters. I was reluctant to meet the two girls, since I was scared that I would be replacing Ashley. I felt I lost Ashley as a punishment; what if we lost these girls, as a punishment from God since I was not supposed to have children?

I was hesitant on meeting the children, but after much consideration, finally conceded. I was tossed with emotions. I didn't want to replace Ashley, but I not only fell in love with Christy, but eventually fell in love with her two daughters as well. As this was occurring, I was overshadowed with guilt because I felt I was trying to replace my daughter. Because of the guilt, I would take the anniversary of her death extremely hard and would distance myself from everyone, starting the week leading up to her death.

I would attempt to pick arguments with Christy as a means to be left alone during that time. I would find ways to spend countless hours at work or deploy all in an effort to avoid being around anyone on the day of her death and on my birthday. I maintained this process for almost ten years until I finally accepted that I was being selfish and distancing a relationship with a family that loved me.

After talking with Christy, Jeff, and trying to counsel and help other families, I realized that I needed to accept my own advice on how to look at the current situation. I accepted that I had three daughters, and that although one was gone, two were still with me that I could share a lifetime with. Accepting this, I think I started to accept that fact that I could move on with my life without losing Ashley, and without feeling guilty that I was betraying her with someone else.

When I finally decided that I would finish this book as a means to help other men who might be experiencing some of the same feelings and frustrations I experienced, I moved closer towards closure. Additionally, I have found that working with other couples, especially talking with other men (when they are ready) who are undergoing their personal grieving process has also assisted me in growing closer to finding closure.

No set time...no set formula...

One of the most tiresome comments I have heard repeatedly given to individuals grieving is that they need to find closure.

No kidding! Is that what they need? The person who just lost someone near and dear to them, the person who is undergoing this whole ordeal, and the wise words someone offers is they need to find closure? Trust me, we all know that we need to find closure. Accepting that we are willing to work towards finding closure is a whole different ordeal.

One of the most troublesome areas that friends and families face is that they want to help. They want us back to normal. They want to see us make it through this process with as little pain as possible. All good intentions; yet, these good intentions often drive a wedge between us and our family and friends rather than bringing us closer. What many fail to realize is that coming to terms with the death of a child takes a considerable amount of time. I have seen couples where one spouse has come to terms and found closure before the other. There is nothing wrong with the other spouse they are just finding closure in their own time. The problem is it can cause friction in a marriage, so understanding individual timelines is important.

There is no set time and no set formula to finding closure. When an individual begins coming to terms with the death of their child, finding closure may not be far away. The question then develops: How does one come to terms with the death of a child? We must be willing and ready to accept that our child has passed away and that he or she is not coming back. Acceptance is only the first step that I had to embrace before choosing to come to terms with my daughters' death.

Coming to terms…

When one thinks of coming to terms, they often think about the terms of a contract that has been written for a deal of some sort. The individual will sit and read through the terms to determine if the terms are acceptable, and then move forward with the deal.

Personally, I first had to come to accept the fact that Ashley was gone, wasn't coming back, and there was nothing I could do about it. I realized that no matter how upset I would become, no matter how hard I begged that she come back, there was nothing I could do that would change the end result. Coming to terms was hard, as the guilt and regret continually crept about rearing its ugly heads every time a questioned the incident that occurred.

I began questioning my actions all the way back to joining the Army. Maybe if I chose a different path anywhere along the road I had traveled this would not have occurred. I dwelled on the different areas of my life I could have done something different that might have changed the outcome. Over and over, I would play back various scenarios, each showing different options I could have chosen, but didn't.

After awhile, I realized I spent so much time thinking of what could have been and becoming angry that I didn't choose those other options that I felt I hadn't moved any further along in my grieving process. Contrary to my thinking, I had moved further along. I needed time to replay various scenarios and come to the realization that I was stuck with my choices and had to live with them. I had to first come to terms with my life, the decisions I had made, and the acceptance that my little girl wasn't returning.

What I had realized was that coming to terms wasn't about the fact that my daughter passed away, but also with the decisions I made before Ashley passed. I accepted the fact that although my decisions may not have been the best, they were the ones I made. I couldn't change them now no matter how much I may have wanted.

This is never an easy subject to digest alone, never mind sharing with anyone. I have spoken with some who look back and regret their decision to marry. In their mind, if they had not married, they would not have had a child, and then the child would not have died. Though I can understand this, especially since I thought that scenario myself, I can speak from experience that even after divorcing, my daughter was still gone and there was nothing I could do about it. Getting divorced didn't help that specific situation. The danger in this line of thinking is that we may become so risk adverse that we never accomplish anything.

Years ago, I met a couple who were going through a challenging time. The husband went from making definitive decisions to becoming extremely hesitant and not making any decisions at all. This left his wife feeling frustrated, since she wanted a partner not a non-responsive adult. Meet Dirt Bike Dad.

Dirt Bike Dad...

Dirt bike dad (DBD for short) was truly into riding dirt bikes. He grew up riding dirt bikes through trails and even competing in some small races. He was practically able to fly with all the adrenalin pumping through his hands when he took off down the trails. DBD would do jumps and crazy stunts that people would talk about for days after riding with him. People would ask to go out riding just for the opportunity to see him flying high over heart pounding jumps and difficult trails.

It was only natural that when his son was old enough he would teach his son to ride a dirt bike. DBD started his son off at an early age, and as he grew people thought the boy was born on a bike. Father and son time always consisted of hitting the trails. They would be gone for hours and hours at a time. Almost every day after school, this youngster would hop on his bike and go for a ride, and when the weekends came around, his friends knew he would be out on the bike. One Saturday evening, DBD had friends over who were sharing stories of some of the crazy antics he had performed in his younger days. His son sat listening to every word with awe, amazed how great a rider his dad was.

The next morning, the boy jumped out of bed early to go for a ride with a few of his friends. By late morning, one of the boys came riding in at high speed to tell DBD that there had been an accident. DBD jumped on his bike and followed the boy to his son. As DBD pulled up, he found his son lying on the ground with a broken neck. The boys told DBD what had happened. He recalled one of the stories shared the previous evening and realized his son had tried to follow in his footsteps by attempting a stunt while in mid air.

DBD blamed himself; he blamed himself for having his friends over, talking about the good old days. He blamed himself for allowing his son to be in the room when the conversation occurred, knowing that his son would want to try some of the thing he heard. He regretted giving his son a dirt bike and for teaching him to ride. DBD traced his anger, his frustration, and his regret all of the way back to when he first climbed on board of a bike. He followed his decisions back and found alternatives that might have prevented the loss of his son. He decided that his decisions ultimately cost his son his life, and he felt he could no longer make decisions.

DBD stopped interacting at that point; he stopped communicating with his wife, and stopped making any decisions. His wife thought this was a short phase and understood that he needed time, and she began making the necessary decisions for the family. Unfortunately, after a few years passed, she felt that she was a single parent, since he would still not make decisions. When we met, she asked what could be done when someone gave up on life after a child passed away.

After she explained the circumstances, she shared that she was exhausted. She had lost a son and now a husband as well. When I met DBD, he was silent. I shared with him my situation. He didn't say a word until I told him how I questioned every decision I made, wishing there was one could have prevented Ashley's death. Hearing this, he looked up, and said he wished he hadn't taught his son to ride, since this was the worst decision in his entire life.

Decisions and guilt...

Coming to terms with the decisions we make is something that is hard to accept on a daily basis, never mind the challenges presented when a loved one passes away. After a big purchase, people are usually happy at first, and then they may question if the decision was the appropriate one. This may be instantaneous, and then the feeling of satisfaction returns. In my house, there is the frustration of purchasing an item only to find out that it went on sale the very next week. In our daily lives we accept that we made best decision at that moment. We are able to accept the decision we made and come to terms with it, or learn from it. Each decision has a reason, and at the time, we elect the best suited for that specific situation.

As parents, we make decisions with the best intentions for our children, with the hopes that they will make the right choices in life, have a better life than us, or will surpass our accomplishments. After losing Ashley, I had to come to terms that the decisions I made were the best ones that I knew at the time, but that realization took a considerable amount of time. There is no instruction booklet; there are no step-by-step instructions showing what the end result will be. All we can hope and pray is that the choices and decisions we make are the best, and our children will learn from them.

When I have spoken with parents who are in this phase of their grief cycle, the most repeated topic we discuss is the intentions behind the decisions they made. Did they try? Did they have the right intentions? Were the decisions made the best at the time? Unfortunately, the frustration and anger sets in with the questions wondering why their child did not listen, or just not do that one thing that may have cost the child his or her life.

Time...

So many times, I have heard parents say they wish they had more time. I wish I had more time with my daughter. I wanted to see her grow up; I wanted to see her involved in activities that I will now never see her participate. I wanted to be there for her when she rode a bicycle for the first time, when she had her heart broken, and to walk her down the aisle.

Those experiences will never occur, and I had to learn to accept those and realize that the time I had was all I will ever have with her. The lesson I took away was to try to give as much time as I could to those I love and try not to sacrifice my time with those individuals. Unfortunately, I am human and I slip from time to time, and as soon as I realize this, I try to rectify the situation. Those who know me, recognize that I attempt to fit 36-48 hours into one day with work, family, extracurricular activities, teaching, etc. Making time for the important things can often be challenging.

We never realize how much time we may have with loved ones. Often, we take for granted that we will have plenty of time with our children later. We accept the fact that our children are supposed to outlive us, and we will have plenty of time with them. Unfortunately, this is not always the case.

Time is precious, and anyone who has lost a child will tell you to cherish the time you have. The challenge we are faced with is coming to terms with the time we spent when the child was alive. Anyone can think of times that we could have spent more time with our child. I know I certainly can, and I lost my daughter at 10 ½ months. Often, a person is filled with regret as they think of all the things they could have done with their child, and all the things they could have done in the future.

One of the hard truths for anyone to accept, never mind someone who has lost a child, is that we can say what we would want to do or would have wanted to do, but hindsight is twenty-twenty.

We don't have a crystal ball; we don't have a time machine that allows us to return to the past. If we did, my daughter wouldn't be dead, I would have won the lottery, and would not be writing this book now. If we did have a way of foretelling the future, we would all make different decisions and spend time on what truly matters the most- time with those we love.

Listening...

Besides desiring more time, the next most common feeling that a parent experiences is frustration, resulting from their child not listening or taking the advice. These instructions include: Don't go out into the street; don't use drugs, don't do that without supervision, don't walk down that street, or any other scenario you think.

I have often heard a parent, especially a father, overridden with guilt because his child just didn't listen to what had been taught. The challenge for the father is understanding, accepting, and recognizing that he did his best and that children make choices too, sometimes with tragic results. Although we may not want to accept this answer, there are times that a child will make a decision on his or her own and the decision will be wrong. We must remember that no matter how strict or lenient we may be with our children they still have a free spirit to decide.

This is a hard fact to accept, since we feel we should be able to make the decisions that would keep our children safe. When we accept that our child has made a decision that may have cost him or her their life, we immediately think this is a direct result of our parenting abilities. I have yet to meet anyone who has deliberately tried to teach their children the wrong lessons in life in hopes that the child would make the wrong decision and eventually die. As a result, we, as fathers and as parents, have to come to terms that we attempted to teach our children the best lessons, the best values, and the best decisions to make in our absence.

Your time...

I mentioned we often wish we had more time with our children. After losing a child, people want us to move on with our lives. For each individual, the time for this has no set schedule. Just as there is no instruction book on how to raise your child, there is no time schedule as to when certain events will occur in your life or in the life of that child. Just as there is no schedule as to when certain events will happen, there is no set schedule for coming to terms with your loss. The bereavement process takes time, there is no set time limit and depending on the circumstances in one's life each man will find closure in his own time.

Finding the closure you desire is going to take time, and is often hard for family and friends to accept. These family and friends care so much about you that they want to see you find closure. Unfortunately, some with good intentions attempt to help you find closure faster than you may want. I had friends who couldn't understand why years after my daughter passed away I was still coming to terms with her death.

Each person, each father, will need to move at his own time and those family and friends need to be both supportive and understanding. There are so many emotions that go through the bereaved parents when closure begins that it is an extremely delicate time. Should someone attempt to rush this extremely personal process, the individual could suffer a setback that takes him or her backward and through the grief cycle again. Each person has his or her own triggers that allow closure to begin, and each person needs to have the time to find those specific triggers. For some, the triggers may be found internally, and for others the triggers for closure may be found externally.

My journey towards closure...

After Ashley died, I had no idea how I was going to handle the entire situation. Frustration continued to haunt me every time I was asked to speak to a family, or a father, who lost a child. As I went through my own grieving process, I started keeping a journal recording my thoughts and feelings as I went through the cycles again and again.

I would start the journal and then rip it up. Start writing again and then rip it up. I must have started the journal that has led to this book at least four or five times, all the while being asked to speak with other bereaved parents in all walks of life. What I hadn't realized initially was that each time I spoke with a father, mother, or a couple I could share my understanding of what I had gone through, which eventually helped them. As I continued jotting down notes, I was asked if I was ever going to publish my thoughts, experience or feelings, since the book could possibly assist other fathers who just need to know everything they are feeling and experiencing is natural.

I am using the writing of this book to bring me closer to the closure. Additionally, I have found that by talking with others and helping them through their bereavement process that I am helping myself as well. I have learned that being there to listen is an extremely important part of the healing process and the grief cycle as a whole. Understanding this, I recommend to bereaved parents to attend a support network when they feel they are ready.

Chapter Ten

Support Networks

After the loss of a child, one should not be surprised that a friend, family member, clergy, counselor, or hospital staff would recommend attending some sort of support group. Some people elect to visit these organized support networks; some choose to embrace support networks established by their church; some lean solely on a small network of friends or family, while others elect not to use a support network at all. Of all the examples previously mentioned, there is no right choice, as each individual must find what is best for him or herself. What family, friends and others must remember is that the choice is yours, and you shouldn't be pressured into attending one if you are not ready.

Ready or not...

Am I ready or not? This is often a question that an individual faces when deciding whether or not to go to a support group meeting. The incident with the counselor left such a bad taste in my mouth; I was determined not to step foot into an organized meeting of any sort where I would be told how I should be feeling. Not only did I not want someone telling me how to feel, but I also didn't want to hear other people talking about how they lost a child and they were moving on. Just the thought of attending would send me back through my cycle of anger and frustration.

Ashley's mother had attended a support group after Ashley died; in fact, it was a well-known organization that has grown into an international organization for the bereaved. At first, she attempted to share with me how supportive everyone was, and how she found others there who were having a difficult time coping with their loss like us. In typical angry fashion, I cut her down saying that I didn't want to be around a bunch of other people who were still grieving or going to tell me that everything was going to be alright. Everything wasn't going to be alright; my daughter was still dead. Hindsight being twenty-twenty, I believe the support group was probably beneficial for my wife, since she seemed to move through the grief cycle faster than I did.

I realize now that I was not ready to sit in a group and speak about my experience or listen to others. I was still at the stage where I had to work through a portion of my anger, questioning and loneliness before I would be willing to allow anyone else in to help me. You, or someone you love may be going through this same experience. They don't want to embrace any type of support network, and would rather keep all of their emotions balled up inside. Although I have learned that keeping all of these emotions balled up is not the best, I understand why someone would and this it is going to take time.

The time that we are looking at is dependent on the circumstances and how quickly a person transitions through the grieving process. Ideally, a person should be ready to step foot into an organized support group, or even sit down with a counselor or friend.

I have met spouses who have asked if I would sit down and speak with their husband. Although I am willing, I first ask if their husband is ready to sit down and talk. The answer, of course, is they think they are, or that he needs to talk with someone. At this point, I have to share with them that we have to allow the man to move through his personal grief cycle before having someone else invade his emotional space. Unfortunately, invading that emotional space can result in delaying the grief cycle that the individual is working through.

After losing Ashley, I was on a slow (maybe a crawl) process of working through my personal cycle when, ready or not, I was thrust into speaking with a young service member who lost his child shortly after I had lost mine. I probably wasn't the best person to speak to him at that time, since I had not even come close to coming to terms with my daughters death, but I could relate to the feelings he was experiencing.

Although I found it somewhat refreshing to speak to someone about being angry, about her passing not being fair, and how I was questioning every decision I had made, I still did not go and visit a support group. Instead, I found refuge in drinking and remaining at work outside of the house. When I finally decided to share something with my wife, she started saying something along the lines of, "in one of my books", or "that in the group"…well, that was enough that had me retreating inwards to my personal cave once again. Bottom line, I still wasn't ready.

Years passed and throughout my travels and experiences somehow or another I ended up speaking with at least a dozen fathers or couples about my feelings of anger, guilt, and failure as a father. I had moved to the point where I could not only speak about my daughter, my feelings and the various stages I had gone through, but I could also listen with understanding about what the other father was experiencing without judging.

One of the reasons I prevented myself from attending a support group or network was the feeling that I would be judged as a bad parent, a bad father who allowed his daughter to die. When speaking with other fathers specifically, I have found one of the concerns they have is feeling they have failed as a father, and, for that reason, many of them choose not to attend a support group. What I discovered years later and shared with people is that you are not judged when you attend one of these groups.

My first time and the importance of not thinking…

There I was standing outside a church, in a large metropolitan city, where this support network was going to meet. I was determined I was going inside, it had been a few years since Ashley died. I had spoken to a few fathers and couples since then, and I had driven a little over an hour to go somewhere I would not have a chance of someone I knew seeing me. Not only that, I even created another name to use, just so no one would attempt to call, email, or follow up with me. All of these were drastic steps most people would consider strange, but for someone who still had not come to terms with his daughters death, I didn't think it was that strange.

Everyone inside was personable, and a few folks came up to find out when I had lost my child and if my spouse was going to join me. I would like to say I remained for half of the meeting, but I don't think I even lasted that long. My problem wasn't what was being said, but my mind playing tricks on me. In the room, I felt as if all eyes were on me. I felt as if people, people whom had lost children themselves, were looking at me with disdain, some judging me for losing a child and others looking on with pity. I'm sure none of this was happening, but I have spoken with others who attended meetings and shared the exact same feelings their first time.

Alright, now that I know I'm normal, I realized that this was my personal challenge of judging myself and not coming to terms with the decisions I made while Ashley was alive. I'm not suggesting that person should wait until they come to terms with their child's death before attending a support group, but I am saying that if you are having some of the similar feelings I mentioned earlier, it could be because you are still working though coming to terms.

What I have accepted is that I can't allow my mind to get the best of me by having me question myself when I am with others. I can't allow my mind to start thinking that all eyes are on me and that I am being judged. What I *can* think is that everyone has been in my shoes; everyone feels as if they are being judged; everyone accepts that we have done our best with our families, and that we want to move on no matter how painful the process may be.

Personal support groups...

Many of us have family and friends who are willing to be supportive while we go through our personal grief cycle. At times, we may hate them; at times, we may love them, and at times, we may feel we are not worthy enough to have them in our lives. In my life, I was blessed with both friends and family who were understanding of my situation, and many of these individuals never attempted to know or empathize with what I was feeling or experiencing.

Simultaneously, I did have individuals who not only wanted to be supportive to me, but also wanted to be supportive on their time and when they felt I needed the support. These individuals over dramatized their emotional involvement and were determined that I needed to share what I was feeling with them. Since I did not want to share, I felt that just speaking with them was more hassle than it was worth, so I moved on without them in my life.

For the friends and family who were supportive, I found they were always there for me. When I was out with them and stumbled upon situations where I felt uncomfortable, these individuals had no problem leaving a store, restaurant, pool, or any other place. When they found out my birthday was coming up, they made it a point to ensure that nothing would be done and gave me the space I needed to be alone. Many of these individuals don't actually realize how much help they were to me, as they provided my own unique support network.

Your Group...

Each of you has individuals who wish to be part of your personal support group. Some of these will be welcomed and some of them will not. How do you know which is which? Well, most of you already realize who doesn't pressure you, who puts up with you outbursts of anger or your silence, who are there when you need them even without saying a word. The majority of these individuals are by your side for the long road, but not everyone.

Think how upset and angry you become, think of how often you ignored someone who has asked if they could help you. There may not be a lot of people willing to stand beside you through the entire journey. I was shocked when I realized the individuals, who were there for me, remained supportive even after I would give them the silent treatment or decide to leave in the middle of dinner with no explanation. If you happen to have recently lost a child or just want friends and family members to understand what you are going through, I would recommend they read this book, so they can understand that you need time and distance.

For those who continue to push you to open up or share how you are feeling because this is what they believe is best; be cautious on how you handle the situation. There are people that it took years for me to forgive or even speak to again after they pushed so heavily for me to open up and speak to them about my feelings. There are those who don't understand what we are going through, or how we are handling our personal grief cycle. Just because our cycle may not be what they recognize as the prescribed path doesn't mean that we are not dealing with it on our own terms.

You or a loved one is coping with the loss you are just approaching it differently than prescribed by others. Your family and loved ones need to recognize this and accept this as part of your healing process. At the back of this book, you will find a handout to give to those friends and family members who don't seem to understand.

In time, people will understand that you are ready to allow someone in, as you will slowly begin to open up and share with them some thoughts or feelings. Hopefully, they will understand not to push and allow you to go at your own speed, and talk when you are ready. You may decide you want to share one thing, but nothing else. The individual listening will need to realize if you open up about something, leave it and don't push further. The challenge for them is to know when he or she is allowed to respond, touch, or what type of acknowledgement you are willing to accept. Quite a bit of this is trial and error. Unfortunately, since we are the ones who are personally experiencing the loss our loved ones, friends will end up bearing the brunt of our emotions. This is where some organized support groups are beneficial, since they understand in a general sense what you are feeling.

Organizational Support Groups...

Organized support groups may consist of two types of individuals. Those who have lost a loved one operate some, and there are those that are operated by clergy, church members, counselors, and psychologists. Each group may be beneficial to you, depending on what your specific need may be. I first avoided any type of support group, because

1)   I didn't want anyone telling me how I should feel

2)   this was my time to grieve and I didn't want to hear anyone else sharing how they were upset by their loss.

Selfish, I know. Yes, I recognized it back then and just didn't care. In time, when I was ready to visit a support group, I realized that if I were going to listen to someone, I wanted to listen to someone else who had lost a child personally. Call me selfish, but I wanted to see if others felt the same way felt.

When I finally visited the support group, I found wives, grandparents, and a father or two, if I was lucky. This could have just been the group I visited; it could have been just the nights that I stopped in, but when I was approached by two women who asked if I had lost a child, they were amazed that I was there.

What I have found speaking with other fathers is that many were reluctant to go to an organized support group, since they shared the same concerns I had. After being in their shoes, I know telling them they will not experience that is not the best approach, because I know I wouldn't have listened. Instead, I share that I had the same concerns, and I didn't want to be around anyone who was either cheerful saying everything was going to be alright, or around someone who just wanted to share their experience or pry into my feelings. My answer is that when your ready you should try it out. I do share that I drove an hour away and walked in saying my name was something different, since I didn't want anyone contacting me later. I have offered to go with others and leave when they were ready. To this date, I have only had one father take me up on this offer.

Two bereaved fathers and the stairs...

During one of my military tours, I had the distinct honor to serve as a course director, allowing me the opportunity to meet and work with many military students from varying walks of life. Each student received a counselor whom they worked with while attending the course. Though I didn't publicize losing a child, the quiet rumblings spread throughout the cadre, when they realized that I didn't celebrate my birthday.

During one of the classes, a counselor asked if I would speak with his student who had an experience with which I could relate. After meeting with the student, I learned he had lost a child, and was on the verge of divorce. We spoke about what he was feeling, the anger he had, the guilty feeling he developed, and the increased guilt he felt as he ran away from his feelings. We talked at various times during the course, and he finally asked if I would accompany him to an organized support group, since he wanted to give it a chance and hear what they had to say. I agreed to go with him, and while we were in one of the cities we visited for an exercise, I found a support group to visit.

If this was a movie, it might have been in a comedy. As we approached the building, we walked up the twenty or so steps to the door when he decided he didn't want to go in, and we walked back down. Upon reaching the sidewalk, he paused, turned around and said he had to do this and back up the steps we went. Before reaching for the door, he paused, turned and said not today, not right now. As you can imagine, back down the steps we went. Two more times we traveled up those stairs, as he attempted to enter the building and go to the support group meeting. Ultimately, he didn't go into the meeting, but the fact that he tried was important enough.

To go or not to go, the choice is yours...

Visiting an organized support group is a choice that only you can decide. Friends, family, and others can suggest attending a support group, but ultimately the choice belongs to you and if you feel your ready. I can share that walking into the unknown environment to talk about your personal situation, or hear what others have to say, can be challenging. Today, I still have trouble walking into anyplace where they have a speaker who hasn't suffered the loss of a child. This isn't fair of me, but I am biased to the point that I prefer speaking to someone who has walked in my shoes and understands exactly what I am going through. I will still speak with counselors, psychologists, and anyone else who will take the time to listen about how I felt and what I still feel, so they can use my experiences working with other bereaved fathers, mothers, and couples.

Chapter Eleven

And now...

What is the next step? What do you do now? The choice is yours on how you will approach your personal grief cycle. You can take the long road; mine has only been twelve years. My path has included numerous bouts of anger, quite a bit of alcohol, contemplated suicide, divorced, distanced myself from friends and family, and volunteering for war time deployments, all as a means to escape coping with or accepting Ashley's death was out of my control.

I spent years being angry with friends and family who were only trying to be supportive; they just didn't know what I needed. I was asked if I would have given someone the handout I created. Well, I can think of at least half dozen individuals that frustrated me enough I would have given handout to without even blinking. This may have prevented the years of not speaking and the awkwardness of trying to patch things again. One person I would have given the handout to was my own mother. After she continued to call to talk about how she was feeling and wanting to know how I was feeling, I stopped speaking to her for about two years.

Even during that time, she purchased ornaments and special collectibles for Ashley, which just rekindled the pain. Think how awkward that was when I decided to make the first call. Some of you may have been there yourselves, you might be there right now, or you may be heading that direction with a family member or friend. Go to the back of the book, pull out the handout and give it to that individual right now.

The next step is to start accepting your own personal grief cycle and work through it on your own time. Let others know you are dealing with your loss, and you need time. Understand that you have the right to be angry, and that you don't have to put all of your emotions and feelings aside to take care of everyone else. Realize that your not going to want to talk to others, and that you're going to want to sort things out in your mind. Take the opportunity to accept that you had the best intentions for your child, and that you tried to be the best parent that you were. Work on consciously accepting, what took me years to realize, that you're not a failure as a father.

In closing...

How do you bring a book to close when the topic is something that you live with daily? I began writing a journal to help come to terms with my daughter's death; that eventually led to this book. Over the past twelve years, I finally was able to speak about Ashley's death without coming to tears or feeling the rage build inside of me. Though I would not prescribe this approach to everyone, I found (for me) that being asked to speak with other fathers about their loss and help them work through their personal grief cycle ended up helping me out immensely by realizing that although I had felt like a failure, I was not a failure as a father.

Acknowledgements

The last twelve years there are many different people that have been by my side and have supported me through my own personal grief cycle. I wouldn't have been able to finish this book without the support of my wife Christy, and my daughters, Elizabeth and Jessica, who have been so patient for so many years and provided me the time and encouragement to not only finish this book, but to develop a workshop for other fathers, mothers, and couples who are facing some of the same challenges I faced after losing Ashley. These three specifically helped me realize that I wasn't a failure as a father and provided me the opportunity to prove that many times. I would also like to thank a few special individuals who have always been part of my personal support group whether they knew it or not: Chris, Kim, Rob, Zane, Gus, Russ, Heidi, and Jeff

A special thanks to my editors Caila Daziel and Andrew Norton for taking the time to review the manuscript, make suggestions and provide the editing so I could take this to publishing.

Handout

Thank you for caring and being concerned that I am not coping with the loss of my loved one. As each individual grieves differently, I wanted to provide you a quick note to share that I am working through my own personal grief cycle. This note will share some of the things I am experiencing and feeling, and when I am ready to talk I will.

1. I am going to be angry for a while. Please don't take this personal, but I am going to be angry and I need to get past that. Please understand that while I'm angry I am definitely not going to want to sit and talk and try to share my feelings. I want to be angry and I need to be angry.

2. I am going to be quiet now. I don't want to talk right now I just need some time to sort some things out by myself. When I'm ready to talk I will; but that will have to be after I work these things out. I can't give you a time frame; but when I am ready you will know.

3. My personal grief cycle is different from what others go through. Because of that I need you to be understanding, patient, and not to give up on me. I have been reading a book *Facing a Father's Feeling of Failure* by Wayne Taylor, which is helping me work through my loss.

4. Thank you for understanding and supporting me through this difficult time.

Made in the USA
Las Vegas, NV
18 December 2021